LIFE TO THE
EXTREME

LIFE TO THE
EXTREME

How a Chaotic Kid Became
America's Favorite Carpenter

TY PENNINGTON

WITH TRAVIS THRASHER

ZONDERVAN®

ZONDERVAN

Life to the Extreme
Copyright © 2019 by Ty Pennington

Requests for information should be addressed to:
Zondervan, *3900 Sparks Dr. SE, Grand Rapids, Michigan 49546*

ISBN 978-0-310-35737-7 (hardcover)

ISBN 978-0-310-35823-7 (special edition)

ISBN 978-0-310-35739-1 (audio)

ISBN 978-0-310-35738-4 (ebook)

Any internet addresses (websites, blogs, etc.) and telephone numbers in this book are offered as a resource. They are not intended in any way to be or imply an endorsement by Zondervan, nor does Zondervan vouch for the content of these sites and numbers for the life of this book.

Unless otherwise noted, all photos are courtesy of Ty Pennington.

Photos on pages 37, 84, 124, 133, 151, and 190 are courtesy of Chaz W. Howard.

Cover design: Curt Diepenhorst
Cover photography: Nete Netvig
Cover illustration: Branislav / iStockphoto
Interior design: Denise Froehlich

Printed in the United States of America

19 20 21 22 23 24 /LSC/ 10 9 8 7 6 5 4 3 2 1

To the amazing humans who believed in me
through so many chapters of my life . . .
even when I didn't

And you may tell yourself, "This is not my beautiful house."

TALKING HEADS

⟶

Lights will guide you home
And ignite your bones
And I will try to fix you.

COLDPLAY

⟶

It is easier to walk through a door than to run into a wall.

TY PENNINGTON

I'M TY PENNINGTON, AND THE WRITING BEGINS RIGHT NOW.

If you've bought this book, then chances are I've been in your home. It sounds kind of creepy, but whether it's my voice or my face, I've probably been in your family room at some point. Maybe in the afternoon with *Trading Spaces* or on a Sunday evening with *Extreme Makeover: Home Edition*. And what's awkward about that is that for some reason, you may feel very comfortable with this. Why? I'll never know. But I do know exactly where you store your unmentionables.

I constantly get people coming up to me saying, "I grew up watching you." You did? When did we meet? Was it in detention? You might have never heard of me if it wasn't for my art instructor at Kennesaw Community College pulling me aside one day after class. Thank God it wasn't to tell me, "I'm giving you an incomplete."

"You realize you're talented, right?" he said.

Up until that point, the only one who had ever commented on my art and design projects was my mom. Sure, some of my work was good enough to get pinned on the fridge, but mostly people had always just said the same thing about me: "Well, you're different. That's for sure." I heard that a lot, mainly in the hallways while I was in trouble and on my way to the principal's office. I had no idea I could turn any of that into a job. Especially a job that would allow me into American homes every Sunday night.

Another comment I've often heard is someone asking me, "You know how lucky you are?" I nod my head and agree, and everybody else in my life would concur. Especially my brother, Wynn. We both know that when it comes to luck, some people can fall off a building and land in garbage, others in gold. I'm one of those guys. The pendulum has swung both ways for me, however, and like anybody's life, things happen around the corner that I never expect. We're all dealt crazy hands that can surprise us in life.

One thing you'll see in my life story up to this point is that you can't trust success. One of the lessons I've learned (sometimes the hard way) is that what goes up can also come down. Everything in life is like a roller coaster. So whenever you start feeling like *Oh yeah, there's no way I can fail*, you better watch out. The season 8 premiere for *Extreme* is a good example of that.

We started the new season in the fall of 2008 by building a facility for Baltimore's Boys Hope Girls Hope, an organization providing at-risk students from rough neighborhoods with a place to stay while going to school. The contractor we used planned on constructing an 11,000-square-foot, modular-built house, the biggest single-family home the show had ever done. It would be built in a different way than usual—the walls would come already assembled, and once they were connected, all they needed was to have the roof delivered. I remember thinking, *That's an interesting way of doing things*, but we'd already had so much success and had built so many houses up to that moment that we felt totally confident.

Who could have imagined that the crane carrying the roof would get a flat tire on the interstate on the way to delivering it? So instead of arriving at 7:00 a.m. like planned, the roof got there later that afternoon. And who could have imagined that a hot summer thunderstorm would come through and fill the drywall—which was already mounted—with three feet of water? We went from thinking we were going to finish a day ahead of schedule to me hanging on to a tarp on the roof while a tornado roared through.

Talk about highs and lows. Life is a lot like building a house in seven days: so many things happen that you can never predict. You find yourself in situations you've never been in, like having to dry out a home that's been flooded before you can resume construction. Suddenly things get put on hold and everything that can go wrong does go wrong. Yet through hard work, creativity, and the help of people working together, you surprise yourself by pulling off the impossible.

Honestly, I'm still surprised I was lucky enough to be a part of a show like *Extreme*, yet I'm not at all surprised by the popularity it had with the public. I think what connects us with the stories on *Extreme* is the same thing that connects us with other people in everyday life—how we can all identify with going through a challenge. Sometimes it's struggling with a disorder. Sometimes it's living with financial chaos. And sometimes it's dealing with trying to figure out how to live life after losing a loved one.

Not only could I identify with the people on *Extreme* because of the struggles they were going through, but what resonated with me was knowing we couldn't cure their problems, yet for a moment we could add something to their life to make it feel better. That's what designing a room or designing and building a house can do. It's not a cure for your problems, but it can make life easier and provide a bit of hope in tough circumstances.

In many weird ways, that's why I'm writing this book—in the hope that somehow in the end, I can paint a funny and familiar story about a troubled kid who overcame a lot of obstacles and eventually found his place in life. Hopefully whatever struggle you may be going through will be made easier knowing that someone who got fired from almost every job he ever had would be the guy leading the charge of do-gooders who would revolutionize television and the way houses are built in seven days. I never expected to be leading this band of do-gooders and to be able to walk away from a job saying that lives were better because of our work.

Lucky? Yes, I've been *extremely* lucky to have doors open and experiences in my life leading me down paths I never saw coming. Because of those experiences, I'm a much better and different man than I was before they happened to me.

Any credit and accolades I've received over the years can be answered by my mom, who quotes one of our favorite movies, *Adis Pozal*, when she sums up her thoughts about my success: "His verbal skills weren't high, but he talked a lot. And listening to him was like trying to drink from a fire hydrant."

I think that really sums up what my childhood was like.

My story is about dreams and surprises and failures and hope. It's about individuals like Kristy Norbert, executive director of Boys Hope Girls Hope of Baltimore, someone you meet who changes your life forever.

"I think as a human being your whole goal should be to affect one person positively," Kristy said on the show. "You do that, you have a great life. This is affecting so many different people. And I feel so fortunate that I'm able to be a part of that."

That's my hope with this book—to affect one person or hopefully many in a positive way. We can make that happen here. So what do you say? Are you with me?

Let's do this! (Said through a megaphone.)

Day

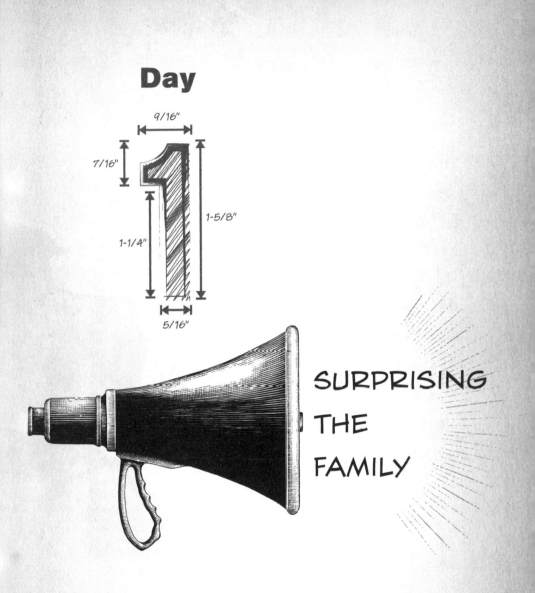

9/16"

7/16"

1-5/8"

1-1/4"

5/16"

SURPRISING
THE
FAMILY

Surprising the Family

Fade in on a shot of a spinning ceiling fan paired with the sound of an Apache helicopter. The camera glides across the ceiling tiles and eventually finds an industrial clock with the second hand keeping time with the rhythm of the blades as Creedence Clearwater Revival's "Run Through the Jungle" starts to creep on beat into the soundtrack over a vintage loud speaker.

Jump cut to a tight shot of sweat beading on a sweaty brow. On closer inspection, create a makeshift headband possibly out of underwear.

Cut back to the war zone with many explosions, flares, smoke, and grenades going off. Close-up shot of a helmet with a playing card under the mesh, then to the face of a jester, and then to the word "Joker." Cut back to the clock and ceiling, panning horizontally over words written in chalk all starting with the same three words:

"I will not . . ."

Jump cut back to the battlefield from the ground view. Fighter planes begin to dive and take aim . . . Close-up shot of the soldiers' eyes getting bigger as the sound of approaching planes gets louder . . . Make a note to try to get all this footage in one pass so we don't waste explosives and time on location.

Oh wait . . . where was I? Yes, right.

They say war is hell, and hell is supposedly a very hot place much like Florida or Georgia in July. I'm pretty sure that wherever hell is, it involves a lot of screaming and yelling, drowned out by loud, unexpected explosions followed by flying debris. All of this causing many to look for cover while a few relish in the chaos, somehow remaining unscathed among the onslaught of, well . . . pure hell.

This isn't a campaign against the Axis of Evil, or even the all-too-real images of lives lost featured on the cover of *Life* magazine. Lucky for me this is neither war nor hell. But this is a battle, one that affects many and one that's fought every day in America. A battle that can be won with focus, determination, and teamwork, and by setting an example as a great leader that others will follow. (None of which I have.)

YES!!! Wow. Just reading that gets me motivated and ready to storm the castle. Let's do it!

Instead of the bugler sounding the charge with his horn, there's a loud ringing in my head that's not caused by distant mortars, but rather a more immediate deafening sound.

The first-period school bell.

It's quite alarming, not just its tone (that will come moments later) but the visual motion picture the visitor will see peering through the rectangular glass in Miss Spaulding's class. There I am in the middle of the blitzkrieg, ducking from incoming fighters in the shape of paper airplanes, launching grenades of my own in the shape of large erasers that explode with powder as they slam against the chalkboard. I'm being outgunned by Johnny and Jamal on my right flank, so I push forward, dragging my desk along the window corridor, hoping to use the teacher's pets as neutral shields. But as in all battles, you will have collateral damage.

Let's face it, considering I am instigating all this while completely naked (this is why I was dragging the desk—I was trying to cover up my "homework" . . . you should've seen the substitute teacher's face), I'm pretty sure the damage will have a lasting impact, especially when I recognize my mother's look of horror as she stands at the doorway. A doorway that, God bless her, she will spend her life trying to unlock. A doorway into the mind and uncontrollable behavior of a child with attention deficit hyperactivity disorder, aka Pandora's Box. (I especially like the *d* for being disorderly.) You see, Mom is studying to be a child psychologist and has come here to test the worst kid in the school.

"Mrs. Pennington," the staff warns her, "are you sure you want to know who that is?"

SURPRISE!

Come to think of it, *surprise* might be my favorite word. For so many reasons.

SURPRISE! I don't have focus, punctuality, or great class participation skills, aka teamwork. However, I can lead the class, just not in a direction that's healthy.

SURPRISE! After I'm born Gary Tygert Burton Jr.—that's right, junior, even though I'm the second son—after seeing his new bright-eyed baby sibling, my brother throws his bottle at me.

SURPRISE! It's what you get if you behave well in class and at home.

SURPRISE! I find out where Mom hides all the surprises, so they're not a surprise anymore.

SURPRISE! "We made breakfast on the couch for you, Mom, thinking it's the stove. Sorry the couch is brand-new."

SURPRISE! I get kicked out of Boy Scouts for biting a kid's ear off.

SURPRISE! I wet the bed again. Looks like we can use some more sheets and a mattress.

SURPRISE! I break my arm jumping off the roof playing army. But it looks very real, like stuntman-type quality. Seriously.

SURPRISE! I get straight Ds on my report card. I'm really getting this.

SURPRISE! I make a new piece of furniture out of the piano's leg. You're welcome.

SURPRISE! I build a three-story tree house in one day by bartering comics. Yeah. That happens.

SURPRISE! I . . . uh . . . we may or may not have set the woods on fire by accident and lied to your face about it. Great news though—no one died. But there are some pretty angry squirrels. Oh, and well, you as parents don't look so happy either. What's that? A beating every day at 4:00 p.m. for a week? Love it. Great idea. That last suggestion is a real SURPRISE. Thanks. Really original.

SURPRISE! I get detention at school every week this year. That's also a surprise. But I sorta see it coming.

Oh yeah. Last but not least . . .

"SURPRISE, JOHNSON FAMILY! We're gonna build you a house in a week!"

"No way . . ."

"No, really. Are you surprised?"

SURPRISED yet? How does that kid end up being that guy?

Uh-oh. I hear a bell going off. Either I'm getting detention or it's something else . . .

"WHO ARE YOU"

That bell I hear is the alarm letting me know we have to write a book in a week. That's right. Oh, and here's what's going to go inside the book: my entire life. Like in thousands of words that are all supposed to be coherent.

Can it be done? Absolutely. Okay, so how do we write a book in a week? Well, I should use the analogy I'm already famous for. What did I do? I built a house in seven days. So I'll divide this book into seven sections. Or chapters. Or maybe parts. Or maybe the parts of sections in each chapter.

So let's start with a foundation. Wait . . . no, I have to surprise the readers first, which I'm guessing is you. Oh, that's right—we already surprised you with my story. And surprise is exactly what's on my mom's face when she realizes that, well, I have a few challenges.

The first challenge begins when she realizes she's giving birth to me. Seriously . . . Would you want to be Ty Pennington's mom?

So pretend I'm standing on a bus talking to you. Can you picture that? I bet you can. So let me start by telling you about the Pennington family.

Let's meet Yvonne Vickery and her two sons, Wynn and Ty. They live in Atlanta, Georgia. Yvonne is a hardworking single mother with two jobs who's also going to school to be a child psychologist. She fell in love with a musician named Gary Tygert Burton, mostly because he was good-looking and she has a habit of falling for musicians. They first have Wynn, and next they have Ty, who will be named after his father. Then hard times fall on Yvonne and the boys.

No, it's not when Gary Sr. leaves them, but it's when she discovers her youngest son is absolutely out of control.

So I'll go back into first person. My mom is a psychologist. She is getting her doctorate in child psychology when she shows up at my school and asks the principal if she can observe the most troublesome child in the building as part of her thesis. (In case you have ADHD and skipped the opening of this chapter, go back and read through it.) The principal thinks maybe this is some kind of weird joke, but it's definitely not. She is serious. The look on her face when she peers through the glass to see that troublesome kid waging terror in his classroom is one I'll never forget, because I'm the one she's looking at. I'm that kid. I guess one positive way to look at this is she doesn't need to do an additional observation, since Lord knows, she's seen enough.

My "big brother" is a year and a half older than me. When I come home from the hospital, Wynn looks at me and then throws his bottle at my head. He suddenly seems to realize that things around the house are going to be a lot different. Much of that attention he's been getting is suddenly going to be sucked out of the atmosphere. It's easy to understand why we grow up beating the tar out of one another.

Dad? Well, that's a bit of a complicated story. Meeting my biological dad comes as a surprise too, since it doesn't actually happen until I'm in kindergarten.

I've just finished a game on the Jolly Roger pinball machine when a stranger comes up to me and gives me a handful of quarters. I don't say anything as I watch the man do the same to my brother. This happens several times as we continue to play in the arcade center in Underground Atlanta while Mom is somewhere next door at the jazz club called Dante's Down the Hatch. She eventually shows up and points to the stranger.

"Do you know who he is?"

"No," I say. "Is he someone in the news?"

"That's your father."

"Cool. Can I have more quarters?"

This is the first time I remember meeting my biological father whom I'm named after. When I'm born, my father sees me and immediately calls me Gary Tygert Burton Jr. It's almost as if he looks at my mother and says, "This one's mine! The other one's yours!" I have to say—I definitely have more of his characteristics than Wynn does, like my skin tone, for example (which is a nice way to say I'm way better looking . . . or that I look like I have skin cancer).

Gary Burton is a dreamer, but he isn't a great parent or a great financier. Some of the best stories I ever hear about him come from his jazz friends, detailing some of the crazy things he's done. Mom, however, will spend a lifetime talking about what a horrible father he was and all the messes he'd made in life. As the son of two jazz musicians, Gary ends up being one himself by playing the trumpet. My father's father is Big Daddy George Burton, a real showman who plays lead trumpet himself but is also the frontman of a local jazz quartet back in the day when big band and swing are still kicking into the early 1960s.

One of the places Gary gets gigs is on cruise ships heading out for ten days. To be honest, he isn't as big of a name or as talented as my grandfather; Big Daddy is the one everyone used to know. Supposedly Gary's mom was named Pookie and was like the Cherokee Billie Holiday. If that's true, you can imagine how interesting his childhood might have been. My father has four siblings, so that's a big family for a bunch of musicians who clearly have no idea what the word *contraception* means. (But jazz is sexy, and clearly the family has rhythm.)

My parents separate when I'm only three years old. The bass player in Gary's band is Nick Pennington, who I'm also half-named after. Nick's loved my mom since the moment he met her, so when things fall apart with my parents, Nick says, "If it's okay with you, I'll take over." He marries my mom, and not long after that, since Nick is super smart, he gets drafted into the army to work on computers during and after training. We're stationed in Augsburg, Germany, and live there for almost two years between 1967–1969. My brother and I create havoc there, playing with all the other commanders' kids and insulting most of their parents . . . which is unfortunate for my dad.

So basically, I'm raised in a military household. Nick, who I'll call my father/dad from here on out as I've always done, is from a different generation, the sort that believes children should be seen and not heard. He's a big fan of W. C. Fields, who once said, "I like children. If they're properly cooked." So the cocktail of stern army dad mixed with out-of-control kid doesn't bode well for any of us.

Of course, none of us at the time know I have this thing called attention deficit hyperactivity disorder (ADHD). It'll be more than a decade before I'm surprised to discover this.

"BIG MESS"

So where was I? Oh yeah . . . that chaotic scene in the classroom.

So my mom is studying to be a child psychologist and goes to my school to test the worst kid in the school, which just so happens to be me! We've covered that. My behavior is never diagnosed throughout grade school and high school as anything other than being a misfit. In those early grades, things are really bad with the chaos I'm creating, but as I get into fifth and sixth grade and move closer to high school, Mom realizes I have a problem and starts to study and use all these techniques to help.

There's no big article or doctor coming forward at the time to say, "I've solved the riddle," so instead I'm given riddles to solve. Those seem to help. As do the tests my mother puts me through, like setting a timer and having me arrange different wooden blocks to make one complete image. Mom learns that even though my "verbal skills are horrible," I'm good at visual puzzle solving. I view them as motor skills in many ways.

My problem in school isn't just the chaos I'm creating that results in spending a lot of time in the hallway and in the principal's office. There's a bigger problem. It's the reason I'm causing all that chaos in the first place—*nothing I'm hearing in the class or reading in books is actually sticking inside my head.* The moment we start going over an assignment, I don't know what the teacher is talking about. I try to read a paragraph but then have to start over and over again and nothing sinks in. I'm too distracted and I'm not interested, so naturally it doesn't resonate with me. Then I never have the correct answer, and I fail and have no idea what the rest of the class is talking about. So what's a guy to do? For me, it's to keep causing chaos.

One way I like to describe ADHD is that it's sort of like trying to play Ping-Pong while reciting the alphabet backward. It's like being at a party where everybody is talking about something you don't understand and have nothing to say about. Are you going to sit there and act like you know what they're talking about, or are you going to throw out an entirely different subject so they can be discussing something you're engaged in? Or are you going to cause a distraction so that whatever they're talking about makes no sense anymore and you're finally doing something fun? That would be my attitude in class—*I don't know what you're talking about so I'm creating chaos so we're not talking about that anymore.*

By the time I get to Cross Keys High School, the teachers have already heard about me from my Ashbury Park Elementary School days. Teachers single me out the moment I walk into a classroom.

"Burton, you're in the hallway!"

"Dude, I haven't done anything."

Maybe they've seen *Fast Times at Ridgemont High* too many times and think I'm Spicoli's long-lost son. (Wait. That hasn't come out yet.)

This is what I figure out about teachers. In elementary school, you have sweet teachers who think, *I love my job and I love my kids*. But in high school, the teachers are so burned out on troublemakers like me that they're basically, like, "You know what? I don't have time for you. You're a little turd, so go straight to the hallway so I can focus on the kids who want to learn."

At Cross Keys High I quickly realize I've already been labeled with terms I just loathe. Ones like *special needs* and *learning disabled*. Whenever I hear those words, I'm furious. "What? Learning disabled? I'll punch your face!" Everybody in the hallways and the classrooms sees me as the problem child. (A great song by AC/DC.) The only solution is to move to a whole different county and school system to start over, which is usually what happens to kids because they end up basically in a correctional school, which is one step away from juvenile detention.

Throughout all this, two things help keep me focused:

1. Putting me at a table where I can draw and color with crayons or put jigsaw puzzles together.
2. Playing soccer and other athletics that involve lots of running.

My brother and I grew up playing soccer and doing most of the scoring. Let's just say we weren't playing in the most elite of divisions. Most of the teams we played against were Boys Clubs with kids with lice and mucus stuck to their faces. Wynn would make the varsity team his freshman year of high school. I try to follow in his footsteps but have a growth spurt that becomes a detriment to my game. Picture the ball soaring through the air to lanky Ty Pennington, who tries to trap it but ends up doing some kind of ungainly robot dance and looking ridiculous. (I'll explain how my last name changed later in the book. If I remember!) All my teammates start falling over laughing, wondering what's suddenly happened to me. So I get benched and then put on the JV team. My grades start sinking. I start listening to Dead Kennedys and Black Flag, and everything begins to tailspin.

I go through some tough years—very violent, angry years—where I want to fight everybody, including those in my family. All kinds of questions begin to arise inside of me about who my father is and what I want in life—issues I think every male goes through, especially when you're facing challenges.

So at this point in my life, it's pretty clear with everybody about how Ty Pennington is going to turn out. They all have a good idea of what the end result is going to be. What you need to learn about life is that sometimes you have to get rid of the big obstacle right in front of you in order to see the future waiting for you. A future with an outcome that's different from what you first expected.

Reminds me of the first time *Extreme Makeover: Home Edition* surprises all of us who are involved in creating it.

"MAGIC BUS"

The best things in life usually aren't created by one lone person, but rather arrive through a combination of different individuals and ideas to make it truly original and authentic. To produce a joyful surprise. This is exactly how *Extreme Makeover: Home Edition* came to be. So yeah, I know I'm suddenly jumping ahead more than three decades later, but just bear with me. We'll be able to go back in time shortly.

> The best things in life usually aren't created by one lone person, but rather arrive through a combination of different individuals and ideas to make it truly original and authentic.

After the success of *Trading Spaces* (think circa 2000), there suddenly becomes this buzz from TV people who want to grab Ty Pennington and do something with him. Purely in a professional sense, of course. The story I'm later told is that there are some of these TV folks sitting around one day watching *Trading Spaces* when an executive spots them and asks them what they're doing.

"There's this carpenter on this show," one of them tells the exec. "You gotta see him. He's really funny."

After a few minutes, the exec seems to agree with them. "Has anybody checked his contract?"

Nobody's thought about that just yet, so eventually this company reaches out to me, and I head out to California to meet with them. After several creative meetings, it's obvious they want to do a show with me, so they put me under contract. They come up with a bunch of ideas for potential shows, and then they ask me what sort of show I'd like to do. I tell them an idea I've had for a while.

"I think it'd be fun to build three-story tree houses and stuff like that for Make-A-Wish kids who are fighting something like cancer or another illness."

Their reaction is less than stellar. "That's nice . . . But nobody really wants to see that sappy stuff."

"All I'm saying is, don't you think it'd be nice to make a show that makes people cry for the *right* reasons instead of the wrong reasons?"

So far, the only tears on *Trading Spaces* have come from people who have been shocked and shattered to see what we've done to their room.

It takes them a while, but they come back to me and tell me they have a show idea.

"So what do you think of this, Ty? We're going to put you with six other designers and have you build a house in seven days. What do you think?"

I think they're out of their minds and have been sniffing glue or something.

"I think it's impossible, but it's a great idea," I say and then quickly add, "But you know it's impossible, right?"

Not long after that, I know we're in trouble when they ask me how much I think it would cost to build such a house in only a week.

"Well, somewhere between $200,000 and $2 million, so you tell me."

Extreme Makeover: Home Edition is initially devised to be a show where people argue and fight about the chaos of making a house in seven days. *Survivor* is a popular hit show that arrives on the scene in May 2000, so this sort of idea makes a lot of sense. The *Extreme* producers even cast people on the show who won't get along in order to help facilitate that chaos, while I'll be the one poking the bear. But surprise, surprise . . . in the process of doing our very first show that doesn't have an identity yet, something remarkable happens, something the producers never expect.

By finding the worst-looking house in the neighborhood, we all come to discover there's a very real story behind that house's condition, one we didn't initially realize. There's a reason the house looks the way it does, with a lawn that hasn't been mowed and a roof that's caving in. The reason is because the family who owns it is spending all their money trying to save their daughter from cancer instead of worrying about the upkeep of their home.

So then imagine a family who is used to seeing me do a makeover of one room. They're not expecting what's going to happen to their house. They don't know we're going to be working with twin builders and completely transforming their living environment, nor do they have any idea that the entire neighborhood will be waiting for them when they come back to see what we've done.

There's the moment on our very first *Extreme* show that I'll never forget. As I greet the family as they climb out of the black stretch limo, asking them how their trip went, the neighbors behind me all cheer and scream and hold up "Welcome Back" signs. The family can't believe all these spectators. I ask them to take a walk with me so I can show them something.

No, I'm not holding a megaphone. I haven't been armed with one just yet.

And no, I don't shout, "Move that bus!" Again, that bright idea will come later.

Instead, we walk *around* the bus, and when the family is able to see their transformed home, they're stunned, overcome with emotion. Their knees buckle and their jaws drop, and they're like "Oh my God!" while they hug one another and me and wipe tears from their cheeks.

I look over to the twin builders and see that they're crying. Then I notice the whole crew is crying as well. I scan the volunteers in blue T-shirts, and they're wiping tears from their eyes. The neighborhood is crying. Even a few of the designers are crying, but that's mainly because they're so tired. And yes, I've even gotten teary-eyed too.

In that moment, I realize something amazing. I know this house isn't going to cure this little girl's cancer, but it is going to provide them a place where they can be more comfortable, especially since they've lost everything. The husband and wife get emotional once they're inside, and so do the daughters, and even the young son weeps with joy. They're laughing and using words like *cool* and *amazing* and *thank you* and *AHHHHHH!*

Nobody has seen my own personal room I've done, so for our young girl, I've designed a dollhouse on an entire wall and a little cubby for her to go through to get to her parents' room and even real grass on her floor.

Suddenly we see something far beyond a show about bickering and beating our heads against the walls as they crumble down around us in seven days. At one point with all this emotional hysteria around us, I look over at my producer with a big grin on my face.

"You see what this show should be, right?"

He nods. "Yeah. We all do."

"I hope that's what we're going to keep doing," I say.

Something incredible has happened. We've taken a fun idea and shaped and transformed it into something truly profound, something that comes to exist out of a combination of different people and events. This is when you know it's true and original and authentic. *Extreme* will turn out to be the show it becomes because of the emotions and reactions of the family. All of us realize it from that very first show.

So wait a minute . . . This can be one of the most amazing shows ever. If you feel this way on our very first show, without any of it planned and predicted, then it can just keep getting better and better and better.

This is why I believe *Extreme* is one of those things you'll never be able to outdo or recreate. The originality of the show arises from an unplanned place. You can't write in a script what's authentic and honest; you can't inject pure emotion into a show, even if you try all day long. No focus group will ever be able to predict or suggest or even point you in the right direction of something like this.

In that same vein, nobody could have ever predicted or suggested I would ever end up figuring out a right direction with my life back when I was a broken-down teenager in desperate need of repair. Yet as I entered college, the bus blocking my view would eventually be moved, and life as I knew it would instantly change.

You see how I tied us back to my story? You're welcome.

"SHAKE IT UP"

It's 1982. I'm eighteen years old. There, I'm helping you with the jump back in time. I'll be doing lots of that in this book, so you have to keep up. There's a rhyme and reason for it, so just be patient. It's like you're looking at the start of a room and wondering how in the world Ty is going to make something out of that. Trust me, I will.

One day I'm sitting in my bedroom listening to The Who when my mom barges in, looking angry and holding some of my illustrations in her hand. To give you an idea of my art during this period of my career, you can see it in my bedroom window. I wanted a silk screen of my guitar hero Pete Townshend, but since I'm unable to find an actual one, I decide to try to create one using my own window screen.

I use glue as paint to create a graphic portrait of Townshend; then once it dries, I assume the paint or ink will squeeze through the small holes still left in the screen. Instead it goes wherever there's glue. After I add the glue and the ink, I spray-paint across the face of it all.

So not only is my parents' window screen a visual disaster, but my portrait looks more like something you'd find in the trash. That's why I give it the title of *Teenage Wasteland*. Not only does the portrait leave you wondering what or "WHO" it might be, but it also makes you wonder why it smells like bug repellent in this gallery. My parents don't purchase the piece; they decide to have me create another piece of artwork. They call it *Replacing the Screen*.

This is the theme of my life in this house. I'm constantly using household items and destroying them to make art out of them. At this point, my parents are basically like *Get. Out. Of. This. House.* So with this as a backdrop to my bedroom, Mom stands at my doorway, holding up my latest drawings.

"Okay, that's it," she says with concern written all over her face. "You're getting help."

I don't understand what's wrong. Why is she so upset about the stuff I'm drawing, like rats carrying wagons full of fingers and other macabre artwork? This is just me going through my dark phase with illustrations, getting my anger onto the paper.

"We're going to see someone," Mom tells me.

So I start to see a shrink named Dr. Gaston Loomis in Atlanta. He's this brilliant doctor who makes me sit down and eat all different kinds of foods, like chocolate, sugar, and peanuts, all while talking with me. He watches my blood sugar and also pays attention to my focus and whether or not I'm staying in the conversation with him. He's kind of a genius at what he does. I remember the loafers he wears are the kind that are soft and have rubber balls on their bottoms. I love those kind of loafers . . . if you're into loafers.

"Your son is the poster child for ADHD," Dr. Loomis tells my mom.

He knows because he has it himself. I can't believe it, because here's one of the smartest people I've ever met and he has the same sort of thing he's saying I have?

One of the most interesting things he ever says still sticks out in my mind. It's about how we're all cavemen, but how there are different types of cavemen. One is a hunter, and the other is the gatherer. The latter is the sort who works in the fields and stores his crops, but the other is the kind who runs out of food and has to go out to kill something in order to eat.

Nowadays ADHD meds are some of the most abused drugs out there. But in the mid-80s, they are still a new thing. Honestly, in an alternate universe I'd tell every soldier going into battle to start taking them RIGHT NOW, because wow . . . Once I'm diagnosed and medicated, I see the world in a whole new way.

One of the first places I can tell how different my brain is functioning is while playing soccer. I've played the sport all my life, but now while playing for Kennesaw Community College the first year they have a team, the motion and activity on the field look different. All of a sudden, I can anticipate where a player's going to be and where the ball will be moving to. I start to read the field for the first time, and I begin to start threading through defenders. I've gone from being a decent player to suddenly doing hat tricks and getting assists. Everybody who's ever seen me play before is suddenly looking with mouths wide open, wondering what happened to me.

You wanna know what's up? It's my brain, and it's finally working. The light switch finally got turned on.

There's a break from the last section to this, so that means I took a deep breath to gather my thoughts and lasso them in. Let me go off on a little tangent for a second about some thoughts on ADHD. Being diagnosed at the start of college is bittersweet, because it makes me wonder how much of the first eighteen years of my education I really missed. When you're young, the mind soaks up everything like a sponge, so what is it about my mind (which seems more like a stone than a sponge) that repels things? I wonder how much I could have learned and the millions of things I never took in. It makes me sometimes wonder if maybe I should retake some of those classes.

I've thought about how things might be different if I'd been raised by two parents instead of just my mom. Yes, my stepfather was in the picture too, but he never was like a real dad because he could never pull me aside and be like, "Look, Ty, you're my son so you better straighten up." I didn't have the firm structure of someone being like that. But then again, maybe I had someone even better—a psychologist as a mom who realized discipline wasn't going to help this, that I needed a better solution. I was lucky I was in an environment where she could tell there was a problem.

So back to Ty at Kennesaw Community College playing soccer with my mind finally working. Two things happen to set me on a different path in life. First off, I'm taking an art history class and doing well in it, and one day the art teacher pulls me aside.

"You realize you're talented, right?" she says.

"I guess, yeah," I say, not knowing exactly how serious the instructor happens to be.

"No, I'm serious. There are a lot of students who come in here, and they can draw, but *you've got it*. I'd hate for you to waste your talent."

"Okay. Cool. Thanks."

This encourages me to start looking at job opportunities in the art field and to figure out what kind of degree is needed to get one. Around the same time, I meet the girlfriend of one of the guys I play soccer with, who turns out to be an artist. And when I use that term, I guess I should say I use it very lightly. She likes drawing unicorns and isn't the greatest illustrator, so she surprises me when she informs me she's starting art school next month.

"You got into art school?" I ask in a nice way that doesn't reveal what I really think about her unicorns.

"Yeah. I'm going to the Art Institute. I got a grant."

This gives me the idea to try the same thing, but unfortunately my parents are just over the income bracket by a thousand dollars or so. But regardless, I still decide to pursue some type of art degree. By now I realize I've always been a visual learner. In school, if I write something down, I'll forget it, but if I draw a picture of what is happening, I always remember it. Like history. If I illustrate a scene depicting what it's about, I'll immediately see it and understand what the answer should be. So pursuing some sort of career in visual arts makes perfect sense for me.

For the next year, I take evening classes at the Art Institute of Atlanta with the goal to become a commercial art technician. The important part of this is that I don't waste my parents' money going to college for four years just to go. I know enough to realize I'm just not interested in that. I know what I'm good at, thanks to the encouragement of my art teacher, so I enter art school, paying my way by painting houses. I'll have lots of jobs that I'll detail later in this book.

In that year at art school, I learn a very valuable lesson in life: the key to success in life is to surround yourself with untalented people so that you really stand out. No, I'm kidding, except that's sorta what happens this year. Initially I consider going to a day school called the Portfolio Center in Atlanta to study graphic design, but the problem (besides the crazy expense) is that one person oversees the program. So at any point during your tenure, they can check your portfolio, and if you're not up to par or if you're behind on something, they can kick you out. Just like that. Three of my best friends go there, and when they graduate, they come out with laminated portfolios

The key to success in life is to surround yourself with untalented people so that you really stand out. No, I'm kidding.

and with actual clients. I'll just say that's not the case with me. I end up attending a night class so I can work during the day.

My class starts with six hundred people, most of whom can barely draw. I realize a lot of these people have been told to come here if they want to change their careers. Sure, it doesn't matter that you don't know the first thing about art, but come anyway, because this is a lot more fun than being a mechanic! I also learn that some of the instructors have their jobs because all you need is to have a job in the field in order to become a teacher. At least at my school. The ideas they end up teaching are broad, to say the least.

"Okay, guys," our teacher announces, "tonight in class we want you to come up with an ad. For anything. For an automobile or business—you choose."

Picture a room of puzzled faces staring back at him, not having a clue what exactly he's asking for.

So naturally, there's only one person in the room who actually speaks out.

"That seems a little broad," I say. "Can you narrow it down?"

"No, no. You can do anything. Use your imagination."

Everybody is stuck because the project is so wide-ranging. Soon I become the interpreter between the instructor and the students, a trait I'll learn I'm quite good at. I like to get people on the same page. You've seen me do that a few times, right? Not only that, but for the first time ever, I begin to excel in the classroom. When they give me an assignment, I deliver not one project but three, not only because I'm jacked up on this new medication, but also because I learn something about creating art. The first idea is usually okay, while the second becomes better, and the third is usually a combination of both and becomes the chosen piece.

Naturally, not everybody is so happy about my motivation.

"What are you, the teacher's pet or something?" someone asks.

"No. But I thought it was a good idea at first and went all the way through before finishing it and realizing it sucked. So I did another one."

At a certain point that year, the teacher even singles me out.

"Yes, obviously Ty is an overachiever on this. But he proves a very good point."

When we graduate, I'm the star student of our class. Yes, our numbers have decreased throughout the year; I end up graduating with seven others. Most of the students drop out or fail or simply realize they suck. Meanwhile, I'm sneaking into the other school my friends are attending, seeing the equipment they're using and checking out books under a different name to use for a short time. When I see my friends' portfolios, I realize how amateurish all of us coming out of this night class must look, carrying these poster boards with acetate covers. Needless to say, my job interviews don't go well.

It doesn't matter about my portfolio; my passion has been fueled, and for the first time ever, I've finally figured out who my heroes happen to be. Ones other than musicians. Someone like Woody Pirtle, an insanely talented graphic designer out of Dallas. Graphic design really doesn't show up until the '80s, so the idea of just making logos and signage is really quite a new thought, and I discover I'm really good at it. Actually, I learn this during my childhood when my mom has me work on different puzzles. Somehow I can see the positive and negative spaces in an image. This will be a trait that serves me well throughout my career.

It's 1983. Suddenly I'm fresh out of art school and starting to pursue a career as a graphic designer. Did I see that coming? Absolutely not. Nor do I see what happens next.

Surprising yourself and starting a new season of life is always such an exhilarating time. It's kind of like the day we arrive at someone's door on *Extreme Makeover: Home Edition* and announce our arrival. Who doesn't love that?

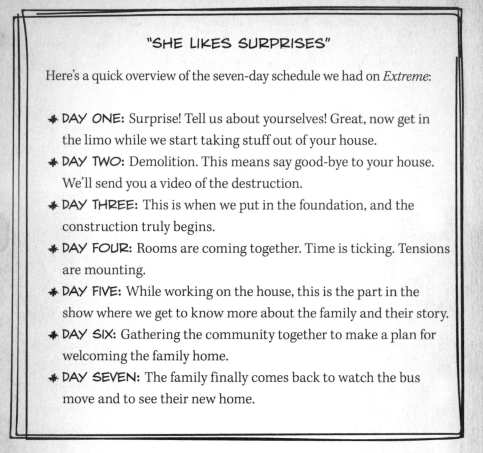

"SHE LIKES SURPRISES"

Here's a quick overview of the seven-day schedule we had on *Extreme*:

* **DAY ONE:** Surprise! Tell us about yourselves! Great, now get in the limo while we start taking stuff out of your house.
* **DAY TWO:** Demolition. This means say good-bye to your house. We'll send you a video of the destruction.
* **DAY THREE:** This is when we put in the foundation, and the construction truly begins.
* **DAY FOUR:** Rooms are coming together. Time is ticking. Tensions are mounting.
* **DAY FIVE:** While working on the house, this is the part in the show where we get to know more about the family and their story.
* **DAY SIX:** Gathering the community together to make a plan for welcoming the family home.
* **DAY SEVEN:** The family finally comes back to watch the bus move and to see their new home.

The two most exciting moments on *Extreme* are when we surprise the family in the beginning and then when we surprise them again at the end when we move that bus. A buddy of mine has a pic from one of our first shows that he posted on Instagram that I love. It's a photo of a beautiful African American family that comes barreling out of their front door and almost fall over each other. This perfectly sums up the emotions felt on that day.

Now, have you ever wondered why these families are literally dressed up as if they're going on some kind of trip? Why don't some show up at the front door in pajamas or looking like zombies? Are they *really* surprised to see us show up? The truth is—absolutely they are. They're not only surprised but also relieved and overcome from a morning full of emotions.

Let's say you're Maria Johnson. You have seven children ranging from one to sixteen, and you all live in a two-bedroom ranch house in Chambonkers, Nebraska. Recently a circus came to town. The elephants got out and decided to march down the street and destroy part of your wonderful home. Since you don't have homeowner's insurance because you put all your money into a nursing home to help your ailing mother, you find yourself broke and desperate. So you and your family send in a tape to *Extreme*.

Now let's say a producer calls you and tells you you're one of the finalists to make it onto the show. Two other families in the Chambonkers area are in the running too. Your kids are ecstatic and nervous at the same time. This producer tells you he has to come over in the morning to get some more video on you and your children, so he tells you to be dressed and have your bags packed. *Just in case.*

The next morning arrives, and you're all wearing the same clothes you'd be wearing to church. A few minutes after the producer and his cameraman arrive, you hear the news: "I'm sorry to have to tell you this, but we picked another family."

There are tears, but these come from the disappointment. For a few minutes, you and your children are absolutely crushed. You had all these hopes and dreams, only to be crushed just like your house underneath those raging elephants.

All of a sudden, an excruciating sound comes from outside the front of your house.

"Good morning, Johnson family!"

The kids beat you to the door as they fling it open and all of you spill out. Ty is behind a megaphone, greeting you with the designers next to him.

This is exactly the way it happens for each family the moment we surprise them. We're really sneaky, right? Actually, it's pretty horrible taking them on a roller coaster of emotions for just a few moments, but it makes for great television. That's why the families you see are always dressed up, even though it's the morning. And why they have their bags already packed. But going from being a finalist to learning they haven't made the show and then to hearing my scream outside their door makes them go bonkers when they see the bus and our crew waiting for them.

There are so many fond surprising-the-family moments to recount in this book. Like the Hardin family in California, where the excited father rushes out of the home screaming, "Yes!" and "Thank you, Lord!" and then comes over to me and shouts, "You must be Ty" before giving me a big bear hug and lifting me off my feet, saying, "Thank you, Ty!"

Or there's the "surprise" wake-up visit with the Walswick family in Yorba Linda, California, where we march with several hundred neighbors down their street to surprise them. Instead of the entire community coming out at the end of the show, they join us at the very beginning.

That day is not just about giving them the thrill of a lifetime, but also about giving us the chance to personally get to know the family, and in doing so, letting America get to know them as well. In the same way I've shared some of my background

> Nobody arrives at a destination without having traveled some sort of road. For the people we work with on Extreme, their road has been long and grueling.

with you in this chapter, we're able to learn about this family and hear the context of why they're at this particular point in their lives. Nobody arrives at a destination without having traveled some sort of road. For the people we work with on *Extreme*, their road has been long and grueling.

Let me share the story of one family whose lives definitely made an impact on all of us on *Extreme*.

"BLOWIN' IN THE WIND"

I'm not sure what to expect or how I will be affected by the project in Arizona. I know the project will be bigger than ever, but the impact that the people, the place, and the experience itself have on my life and how I view it is not only surprising; it's a completely eye-opening experience.

It's April 2005, and the crew of *Extreme* is getting ready to shoot what will become episode 24 of season 2. The country is familiar with Private First Class Jessica Lynch, who at the very start of the Iraq War is injured, captured, and held captive for a week before her rescue. Her story captures the nation's interest and heart, yet Jessica contacts us, wanting the world to know about Lori Piestewa and her heroic story.

Lori is a wonderful mother, an incredible friend, and a brave warrior. She is the daughter of a Vietnam veteran and the granddaughter of a World War II veteran. Simply put, she is an incredible human being. She doesn't have to participate in the invasion of Iraq due to an injury, but she wants to be there for her battalion and for her roommate and best friend, Jessica Lynch. Lori becomes the first Native American woman to lose her life in the Iraq War.

Lori and Jessica make a pact with each other before they leave. If one of them doesn't come back from Iraq, the other will take care of the other's family. Jessica is already close to Lori's family because that's all she talks about and the family visits their training camp and base regularly. As the proud mother of two kids, Lori joins the military to get an education and make enough money to support her family. Her dream is to give her parents a house they can finally own.

Jessica lives up to her end of the deal, asking us to help her make Lori's dream come true.

The moment I see the land in Arizona, I know this is gonna be special. The mountain and desert landscapes are absurdly breathtaking. As the bus, vans, and crew convoy our way through the desert, heading north to the Indian reservations, I'm overwhelmed by the task ahead of us.

Wow . . . we're really going to a reservation to help the family of a Native American woman who gave her life for this country.

Being one-fourth Cherokee (possibly . . . the jury's still out), I am very aware of the sad treatment and history of many tribes of Native Americans, especially the Trail of Tears. They are the ultimate minority— the original Americans—who got a raw deal. I have always wanted to learn more about their culture, the people. Now I have a chance and hopefully can help shed some light on a proud people many don't know much about.

A sign outside the bus window—"Indian Reservation, Alcohol Absolutely Prohibited"—tells me we're getting close. Jessica is riding with us in the bus as we hear the Piestewa story. As I tell the design team why we're here and play the family's videotape, I'm amazed at how much you can really "feel" about someone and how their inner self (soul) can come through by merely watching a video like this. We are heartbroken as we hear how Carla and Brandon have lost their mother and how Terry and Percy are coping with losing their only daughter. The parents' emotion is especially overwhelming, seeing how much they loved and missed their daughter, and seeing them slip up and call their Carla by her mother's name since she looks and acts just like Lori.

Needless to say, after watching the family on tape, we are all deeply affected emotionally, not to mention amped and ready to give them an early-morning wake-up call with the megaphone. There's nothing like that moment when you get to give the family the "surprise" of a lifetime and make a dream like Lori's come true.

Since Jessica is practically family, she joins me as we both scream "Good morning, Piestewa family" into the megaphone. The expressions on the family's faces are priceless. They're shocked to see us and so happy that Jessica has joined us.

"I wish Lori could be here to see us," I tell her father, Terry.

"Oh, she is. She sent you."

I nod, knowing Native Americans believe that when a loved one dies, they don't go away. Their spirit lives on in everything around us— the trees, the land, the flowers, the birds, everything. In fact, Lori's mother, Percy, tells me she loves gardening and planted a cactus around the time Lori's body came home from Iraq. It's never bloomed until the day before we arrive, and sure enough, it blooms with a yellow flower. It's a sign from Lori, Percy says, since the yellow is in support of the troops still in Iraq. We're told that the day we arrive is exactly two years to the day that her body arrived home for a sacred burial.

The week in Arizona is a magical time. Getting to know Terry and Percy is the greatest gift. They are such wonderful people, so proud of their daughter, and raising Lori's children the best they can. It is hard to believe what we all accomplish in seven days. Not only do we make Lori's dream of giving her family a house of their own come true, but we also build a veteran's center for so many Native Americans who have served our country and put their lives on the line. Men and women who are proud to be Americans. Sometimes words can't express the emotions you feel when you see so many faces and hear the stories of people who have lost loved ones who were never recognized or honored for their sacrifice.

Before we open the doors to the veteran's center, we have a ceremony. It is beautiful. Three Native Americans lead the procession, with two on horseback and the other walking next to a horse without a rider, symbolizing the warrior who didn't come back from battle. It's such an honor to look at those faces and welcome them into a dwelling of honor and respect. Our team members Preston Sharp and Ed Sanders do an unbelievable job really making something wonderful happen.

The wildest thing happens the minute we start the ceremony. The winds start blowing like crazy, and it becomes a dust storm. You see, Native Americans believe that when the wind blows, it's the spirits of their ancestors and loved ones coming back to visit. Well, I tell you what . . . We have quite a lot of visitors paying their respects because the wind blows harder than I've ever felt. Too bad I have to ride in a helicopter to get back to the Piestewa home to finish the house and bring the family home to see the house Lori always wanted for them.

Before the family shows up, however, a dog arrives on the site where we want to build the house and never leaves. Every day I show up, the dog is always barking at me. EVERY SINGLE MORNING. I'm always arriving fifteen or twenty minutes late, without fail (no pun intended). I'm thinking, *What's this dog's deal?* So one morning, a Native American on the reservation hears me talking about the dog.

"Don't you know? That's Lori. Barkin' at you for bein' late."

"What?" I ask as I start to laugh. But he's dead serious.

"Her spirit is in the dog. She's saying, 'It's about time you showed up! We've got work to do!'"

Nothing compares to the moment when the family enters their new 4,000-square-foot home. We've built a room celebrating Lori and her life, with photographs, belongings and mementoes prominently displayed. The Piestewas can feel Lori's spirit and look around to see her story unfolding with writing on the wall and the warmth of a courageous life. Of course, the kids need their own specially designed rooms, so Brandon has a Lego theme, while Carla has a princess theme.

Once again, *Extreme* surprises me in those seven incredible days. What's totally amazing is not only what we accomplish but how we accomplish it. It takes so many people coming together to make it happen. It is the Hopi working with the Navajo, who've been at war for five thousand years, and it's the state of Arizona working with the Indian reservations. All these people working with us, not to mention Jessica Lynch, to make Lori Piestewa's dream a reality. And to honor an American hero. It takes so much for everyone to make something this big happen. It not only takes patience and hard work, but it also takes trust, which isn't easy. And yes, it also takes a whole lot of believing that we can all make a difference.

That week in Arizona, I'm surprised by all the things I learn. I learn about HONOR. I learn about RESPECT. I learn about MYSELF, and I learn about OTHER PEOPLE. I learn about other CULTURES.

I learn we are all human beings, whether we are black, yellow, red, or white. We share every day together. The air, the water, the lands. We can do more together than we can apart.

We can do more together than we can apart. I learn about LOVE. Unconditional LOVE.

I learn about LOVE. Unconditional LOVE. We are *all* Americans, and that's what makes us Americans—being better people *together*.

... And that is why I've taken this moment to announce my decision to run for the candidacy for the president of the United States of America! (Well ... not yet!)

"NORWEGIAN WOOD"

Since I ended the last section with such triumph and inspiration, I wanted to wait a second to share this epic fail related to the Piestewa family. See, that wonderful pendulum of my life is always swinging back and forth. One second I'm feeling unconditional love, and the next I'm feeling like a complete moron.

While working on Terry and Percy's room for the Piestewa episode, I set out to be honest to their culture, their heritage, and their spirit. Not only did their daughter give her life for our country, but our country has mistreated the Native Americans, so I take this room very seriously. My goal is to pay my respects to them and make the best bedroom I've ever made.

The piece I'm most proud of in their room is the beautiful headboard, where I created pinions from pine tree limbs so it looks like pieces of teepees that you'd stack and drag behind you when you move. And by the way, here's a little-known fact: The Native American tepee is to this day the strongest, fastest, and most efficient mobile home ever designed. They literally break down and can be set up within an hour; you've got a fire and a home, and, boom, you're good to go! So I build a beautiful bed, and it looks awesome in the rustic environment with its stunning Navajo blankets.

So two months after working with the Piestewa family, I see them at a party celebrating *Extreme*. They greet me with their wonderful enthusiasm.

"Hey, Ty! Good to see you."

I'm excited to see them again and eager to hear about how they're enjoying their new house.

"By the way, did we tell you?" Terry says. "We met your friends."

"You met my friends? Who are they?"

"The beetles in the wood headboard you built. They all came out, about six hundred of them. The first night we stayed in the bed!"

I stand there in shock and amusement and horror.

I didn't smoke or cure or fumigate the wood. And all those pine beetles… yikes.

I assumed beetles only chewed on dead wood, not realizing they're in live trees. Sure enough, after the wood dries up, the beetles all emerge from their homes and begin to start chewing.

Epic fails are part of the surprising aspects of DIY shows. I have a hundred stories like this. They're like the greatest novels ever written, with titles like *The Sound and the Failure*, *To Fail a Mockingbird*, *A Room with a Fail*, and *The Failure in the Rye*. And of course *The Quest for the Holy Fail*!

"ORIGINAL FIRE"

So here's my summary of surprises. Not only was I a big surprise to my mother and brother, but I eventually surprised myself by getting to do what I love on shows like *Trading Spaces* and *Extreme Makeover: Home Edition*. As it turns out, the element of surprise has always been a big part of who I am and how I approach my art. There's also been a certain amount of competitiveness. That's why I've loved *Trading Spaces* so much. Sometimes you'll think, *Okay, this designer used feathers to make over that bedcover, and isn't that clever?* and then you'll think, *Well, if they did that, then I need to do THIS.*

This is one of the things I love about Hildi from *Trading Spaces*. If anybody's done anything even remotely similar to what she's planning, she won't even come close to doing it. She never wants to copy anything or anyone, and in a lot of ways, I'm the same way.

That's what's so much fun about design. When they say every idea's already been done, you know what, it probably has been. But there's always a way to redo something that's never been done in that way! My biggest fear with redoing a room is trying to find a way to make it completely different but then at the end finding out it's really not that mind-bogglingly original.

Always adding one special ingredient that is unexpected and that surprises others—I live for that. I love seeing stuff that's surprising and unexpected and jaw-dropping. Sorta like my life.

Day

DEMOLITION

Demolition

"FIRESTARTER"

'm known now as the demolition guy from *Extreme*, but to be honest, demolition's always been a big part of my life, especially since I destroyed every piece of furniture in my family's house. My brother has destroyed many bathrooms in his life, and to this day, he's still destroying them . . . it's a gift.

It's hard to say what I love more—building and putting things together, or the art of destruction and demolition, aka tearing things apart. From an early age, I develop quite a talent for demolishing almost anything. There's my shattered and tattered crib that will be constantly pummeled by my Olympic-style attempts at gymnastics, such as running down the hall, leaping, and then launching off the couch into a full flip and twist before almost sticking the landing inside my clearly junky, hand-me-down crib.

Then there's the leg of my parents' piano that I decide to rip off and use as a brace for a simple cardboard fort. And of course I can't forget my mother's brand-new sofa that I decide to make breakfast on. It's a beautiful gesture, complete with four eggs over easy, pancakes, and bacon you can almost hear sizzling. Except, of course, for the fact that they're all resting on a couch instead of cooking on a stove. Yeah, my brother even helps me with that one. Clearly, we are too young to notice the difference, or then again, maybe we're just too indifferent to care. Considering we're on food stamps, aka broke, my mom is thrilled to have to buy more eggs and bacon, not to mention to have to purchase another less delicious couch and pillows. Ahhhh, yes.

Once you get a taste for demolition, it's hard not to crave more. However, you have to know when your addiction to demolition gets out of hand and when you need help. For me, it's when my brother and I burn down the forest behind our house.

Picture me, an eight-year-old kid, sprinting back to a place I'd left my brother moments ago. He was kicking dirt on a small campfire we made inside the hideout we called Devil's Cave. It's really just a small, hidden, and camouflaged retreat inside a gigantic, hollowed-out thornbush. My first surprise is realizing that making a fire inside a bush leads to problems quickly. Now as I return to that spot, my second surprise is to discover the fire extinguisher I sprinted home to retrieve isn't going to help anymore.

Yes, that rush of adrenaline is really kicking in now.

As I jump over a dry creek bed and reach an opening in the trees, I see something you really only ever see in epic Hollywood movies like *Gone with the Wind*. My brother sees it too as he stands motionless and helpless nearby. A wall of fire engulfs every tree in the forest, literally lighting up the sky as it races upward toward the canopy. The flames are spreading throughout the woods behind several families' homes that are now in danger of being truly demolished by actually burning to the ground.

Wynn looks over at me, and the fear in his eyes levels me. *What have we done, Ty?* It's the worst expression I've ever seen, like he's about to cry but too scared to. We instantly take off running for help. To call the fire department. Which we scream to my parents, who by now have seen the flames and smoke from our house.

Thankfully the firefighters show up and risk their lives to save not only the forest but also the neighboring homes. Once the flames go out, everybody starts to wonder how the fire started. Wynn and I are still in shock, and of course we say we didn't do it. How could we? We're just kids. My father, being a little more inquisitive, decides to investigate the scene of the crime. Among the ashes he recovers a pack of matches from a jazz club called The Ambassador. He's familiar with this spot since he plays bass there almost every weekend between smoke breaks. Let's just say the evidence is not only a clue but a perfect match as to who may have been lighting up in the bushes.

After my father spends relentless hours of doing a Nazi-style interrogation on Wynn and me, we are finally coerced into confessing. Boy, does he come up with a remarkable punishment. First off, we have to go apologize to the men at the fire department. I still remember the moment as we're standing there crying when the fire chief says, "It takes a brave man to apologize." Then Dad grounds us to our room for a month. And every day for a week at 4:00 p.m. after school, we receive a hard butt spanking.

The brilliance of this is the horrible fear of anticipation, the dread of knowing what's coming. Not to mention the sound of the belt snapping. To this day, whenever I hear anything that sounds like the piercing sound of a leather belt snapping or popping, I crap my pants a little. Clearly the discipline is very effective. It's almost as if Dad was trained by secret operatives somewhere in Eastern Europe. Safe to say, we never started another forest fire after that.

But the rush of adrenaline at seeing something destroyed like that never leaves me. Demolition becomes a secret thrill that's just waiting dormant until it can be unleashed again. I also learn a lot as a result of this epic disaster:

* Smokey Bear isn't going to help you put a Band-Aid on the raised welts on your red and swollen butt cheeks after your daily whipping. And that's a big letdown.
* It's not cool to be a "fire starter," whether they're rumors, accusations, or an actual fire. That is how you get your rear royally beat (cue that late '90s song by The Prodigy).
* Small fire extinguishers are basically useless, except for an occasional burnt toast flambé.
* Some big ideas can go up in flames. But if you're going to light it up anyway, make sure to have a way out of a burning inferno, aka be prepared for the worst. (Oh yeah, and also be prepared for your brother to always fold under pressure of interrogation. So keep your plans on a need-to-know basis.)
* If you're going back for the fire extinguisher, bring a video camera to capture the pure chaos and mayhem, because no one will ever believe or understand just how insane it really is.
* The biggest lesson: make sure to look into padded underwear in case this somehow happens again.

Speaking of happening again, demolition seems to always be happening again and again on *Extreme*. Good segue to the next section.

"BREAK ON THROUGH (TO THE OTHER SIDE)"

My phone is blowing up from all the calls, texts, and emails I'm ignoring, but they don't understand. I have six more days left to finish this book, not to mention a hundred other things going on with multiple projects.

The word *multitasking* is used a lot, but it really is an amazing feat to pull off. Let's face it, if anyone knows all too well about taking on more than one task at the same time, it's someone with ADHD. Of course, in that case the task usually gets left unfinished once a new and more interesting task comes along. That's really where the challenge lies.

The good news for me is that this is the Demolition chapter, and if there's one thing in this world that I love and find interesting, it's destroying things.

There aren't a lot of different ways to smash and flatten a home, but we seem to find new and creative ways week after week on *Extreme*. In fact, it happens a little different each time. But there's always one constant during every house demolition: I'm going to destroy a toilet. That's right. It's just not enough to see backhoes and excavators crunching and devouring a home. No, there must be the sight and sound of a sledgehammer cracking and crushing the crapper like a, well, can. This is why I always wear eye goggles! Otherwise, hello Ebola, E. coli, and other vowel-heavy, flying fecal matters.

There's something about wrecking toilets that provides such a rush. Maybe that's just my juvenile sense of humor. But on *Extreme* we also get to tear down every single room in the house and see the entire structure disappear. Now that's just crazy fun. Especially sending the deserving family a video of us shattering everything from cabinets to windows to doors and floors. (We actually do a lot of recycling too. And we give away materials and pieces to those in need through Habitat for Humanity and other organizations.) On *Extreme*, the house demolition becomes the funnest part of the project. We destroy or maim a lot of homes, but we also come close to maiming ourselves in the process.

There's something about wrecking toilets that provides such a rush.

Like in Oakland when I'm standing on a gigantic crane, a hundred feet in the air, overlooking everybody, and I think, *What if this thing snaps?* Or the time I plan for the house wall behind me to land two feet away from me while I'm talking to the family on vacation. As the excavator's wide mouth swings down on the roof, the wall crumbles, yet I stand my ground. That's a moment when even the cameramen are realizing, *This guy is freakin' crazy.* The shots look amazing, but could we have all been killed at certain moments of the show? Absolutely. How many rooftops have I been standing on, yelling into the camera while someone else is demolishing a nearby section? There's always a tornado of chaos, and if you can capture it, that's gold for television viewers.

I can't count how many times we tried to pull down the house with rope and cables, which is absolutely the most dangerous and stupid thing we can do because something's eventually going to snap. We score all these two-by-fours and wrap a cable around the house, and then we have these backhoes trying to drag it. But almost every single time, the cable snaps, and we're running away in terror, screaming, "Somebody's going to die!"

There are so many times that I'm not just close to getting injured, but I'm literally close to losing my life. I'm always putting myself wherever things are being destroyed and looking for debris flying by that I can film myself talking around. For example, in one demolition in Tennessee for a medic soldier, Paulie's in the kitchen using a sledgehammer on the cabinets while I'm recording myself talking to the family. Paulie swings his sledgehammer so that it strikes the cabinet and comes flying toward my head. I'm hit and there's blood spewing from the gash on my temple, and since the homeowner is an Army medic, I scream out, "I'm hit!" as if I'm on the scene of battle. I also tell Paulie to maybe swing *away* from me the next time while he apologizes. I end up getting stitches for that injury. But honestly—I'm amazed more people aren't wounded during our demos.

Think about it: imagine inviting a hundred people over to your house to have a demo party! So, everybody's slamming their sledgehammers through walls without having any idea what's on the other side of it. I've been talking to the camera numerous times when a sledgehammer blasts through the wall behind me. "Hey, guys, I'm on the other side here!"

Another favorite demo of mine takes place in North Carolina. We decide to have a demolition derby with real, authentic derby cars and drivers. It's nuts. Somehow the show gets the town to turn the park across from the house into a derby track, so while I'm talking to the family just before we demolish their house, I'm in the middle of all these beat-up old cars, along with a cameraman. These drivers have never worked with us before, so honestly, we almost get killed. My cameraman is a big, burly Norwegian man, the Brawny Guy, and he's almost hit, and we're yelling at the drivers to be careful.

Then I get one of my bright ideas—I find the nearest car, jump in, and start recording myself.

"Hey, family! Guess where I'm at!"

The driver looks over at me with a serious gaze. "Son, you got in the wrong car. This is the real deal. This ain't no fake TV stuff."

Seeing the look in his eye and hearing the tone in his voice make me immediately wanna get my butt out of this vehicle. "Hey, man, it's okay—I can—no, wait, no . . ."

"Hang on, son!"

He floors the gas, and in just a few seconds we plow into another car. Thankfully I'm wearing my safety belt. But the impact is so hard that my camera hits my face, cuts my nose, and falls onto the floor. So while blood is dripping all over me, I'm leaning over trying to pick up my camera when, BOOM, another car pounds us from behind. That safety belt I'm wearing? It actually ends up breaking my ribs.

That's not even the craziest moment from the derby car demo. For the final grand-slam climax, one of the derby cars will drive into the house to start the demolition. So the driver rams his vehicle into the front and somehow hits it just right, because a post on the door goes straight through the window. Fortunately, the driver ducked just before the crash. Otherwise, the post would have decapitated him. The shot looks amazing—and yes, this is what I live for—but all I can think is, *Thank God he didn't die!*

I always loved flirting with death on *Extreme*. That's another reason they can't do a show like that now; back then, we used to get away with murder. We literally blew the roof off home improvement TV. And, oh yeah, we also blew up a house with 360 sticks of dynamite in season 5.

Picture tranquil and peaceful Cheyenne, Wyoming. Meet the Miller family, who run a mission that rescues hundreds of abused and abandoned animals. In 2003, they buy a twenty-acre lot with plenty of room and privacy. It also contains a berm house—a home built partially above ground and the other part buried in the earth. Six months after living in their new home, the two Miller children start getting sick, and after trying to figure out what's wrong, they get the house tested and discover it's infected by radon. The gas is one you can't see, smell, or taste, but it's poisonous. The Millers can't sell or refinance the house, and they can't afford to fix it, so they're truly in a helpless situation that we're delighted to be able to fix.

Dan Miller opens up to me about how regretful he is for buying the house and letting his family down. There's nothing like being able to tell him that all of us make decisions we regret—if he only knew how many I've made. We're going to help their family out, and by doing so, I'm going to finally be able to fulfill a lifelong dream—blasting a house to smithereens.

There's something so invigorating about finding a house with no neighbor on either side of it, allowing us to do whatever we want to in tearing it down. I remember being in the house and putting dynamite sticks throughout. "Hey, just be careful with that," someone tells me. I'm the guy they tell to watch out mowing the lawn, so now I'm surrounded by 360 sticks of nitroglycerin. I can't believe we're actually doing this.

One of our cameramen is camped in a nearby tree with a bird's-nest view, his camera covered by plywood in order to get the zoom shot of the explosion. We're in the back, a hundred yards away, and they allow me to do the deal, pushing down the lever. When the house erupts, you literally see the ripples coming across the wheat as the earth shakes. The feeling of blowing up a house—there's nothing like it. I can't fathom how all those two-by-fours disintegrate into dust.

You know you're on an awesome show when you're the ringleader for detonating a structure in front of a crowd of people while holding a video recorder and screaming, "Fire in the hole!" It doesn't take long before I wonder how we're ever going to top that. The truth is we can't; there's nothing that will ever compare to this demolition.

Demo is a very big part of *Extreme*, so instead of creating big explosions, we create bigger experiences and amusing stories to set the context of the scene. And by *amusing*, I mean stupid, and sometimes strange. It gets to the point where the producers will approach me to talk about the demolition, and I'll literally say, "Don't even tell me, 'cause I don't want to know." They know what my opinion will be before they even tell me about their crazy idea.

"Ty, you're going to love this . . ." But we all know I'm probably not going to love it. Like in Tampa, for instance, when we've clearly run out of ideas. Picture a gigantic pirate ship on a flatbed truck heading down the highway and then racing down a street. Then imagine a bunch of Tampa Bay Buccaneers fans dressed up as pirates running toward a house with me talking to the family in the camera: "You're not going to believe this, but pirates are about to demolish your house!"

What the family and the viewing audience don't realize is that a lot of these pirates have been up drinking for three days. I'm just wondering how they came up with that idea in their brainstorming meeting.

"Hey, I know how we can get six hundred drunken pirates! Can we work it into the story somehow?"

"Absolutely!"

Isn't TV great? Well, our show really is great because of the real story behind this episode. *Extreme* is here because of a total freak accident—a plane crash-lands and runs into a house. The pilot is killed, and thankfully nobody from the family dies. The mother witnesses the event while inside the house, and she even attempts to save the pilot before the house erupts into flames. All that fuel keeps the fire burning for hours and even the fire department can't control it. Not only does the family lose everything, but for some fluke reason, they don't have homeowners insurance. So life as they know it is over.

For this home, we have to do a ceremonial demolition with the raging sea rovers and then an actual legitimate one with professionals trained in the cleanup of contaminated areas. Normally when you demolish a house, you simply take away the materials without a problem. But in this case, we realize that to get this right for the family, we're going to have to dig up the dirt since it's been drenched with jet fuel. When it's all said and done, ten truckloads end up hauling away sixty tons of contaminated debris

The great thing about demolition is that it creates work. This helps when you have several hundred people from the community who want to help in some way or another.

"Okay, great. Grab an axe and come with me. Let's find something we can demolish!"

The truth is this: I've been wrecking things in my life beginning in my childhood. Not just walls and windows and furniture, but people too. Starting with my wonderful mother.

"ANOTHER BRICK IN THE WALL (PART 1)"

Remember the demolition scene of me in the classroom? After Mom witnesses the carnage of Ty in the classroom, she knows something's got to give, and she can't put me out on the street. No, she'll wait until I'm a teen to do that. This is 1973. I'm nine years old, and the doctors never talk about kids with attention deficit hyperactivity disorder; instead the doctors tell my mom I have what they call "minimal brain dysfunction."

Thankfully Mom declines to share that little description with me, but she still knows she has to do something. Putting me on Benadryl just makes me drowsy, so after lots of study, she discovers a type of behavioral therapy that she tries on me—first at home, then at school, figuring this can help make things easier for my classmates but also to help me try to improve my grades. This therapy is called the "token economy" system.

Anytime I stay focused for a short period of time and obey my mom, she gives me a token that I can store up and eventually cash in for rewards. A dozen might give me more time to play or earn me a prize. After a while, Mom persuades my school to do the same. So every day, I'm given a sheet that my teachers have to fill out, grading my class participation and conduct as excellent, good, fair, or bad. Every time someone marks it, I feel like a complete moron. Honestly, any time you need someone else to mark a box for you in life, you feel like you're in juvenile detention. Like they're deciding if you get recess. This is the beginning of what life in prison is like. "Score good points, and you're able to get in shop, Ty!"

At the end of each week, if I get good marks, I receive a surprise. After the second or third week of seeing Mom go into the bedroom and come out with a toy, well . . . there goes my motivation, and my slide right back into bad behavior starts. I figure out where the bag of prizes is stored in the closet, so there goes that game. Once I already know what the prizes are going to be, I'm not so impressed. So back to square one.

One day I catch my mom crying in the hallway. She's not only working a full-time job during the day but another job at night, plus she's going to school and trying to raise two boys, with one of them particularly out of control. This is one of those afternoons when I'm losing my mind, causing chaos and running around the house destroying stuff, and I guess my mom simply can't take it anymore. But seeing her nearly keeled over with tears running down her cheeks makes me stop in my tracks.

> *I really am a nightmare.*

Seeing my mom reach her breaking point gives me a breakthrough revelation: *I really am a lot to handle.*

It's not just that Mom is working two jobs and going to school and raising two boys. She's also putting a ton of focus on me, because clearly I have what's been called a *learning disability*, a term that to this day I think is one of the worst phrases ever uttered. She's trying to do her best to figure out how to improve my behavior and my grades so she can stop people from saying I need a better school to handle me—one of those schools for boys who behave badly, one that doesn't lead to good ends. Mom's problem is that she just doesn't have the time and energy to devote to me. I'm the Energizer Bunny, and nothing is working to slow me down. I'm not growing out of this annoying behavior.

Seeing my mom weeping and kneeling on the floor, I have this blank feeling inside me. I watch her put her head in her hands.

"I just can't handle you," she says.

I tell her I'm sorry while I wonder what I'm going to do. I wonder if I'm really this bad.

Even though I'm young, I realize Mom is the only person standing up for me. Nobody else is doing that. Everybody at school is telling her to send me somewhere else. And my stepfather, Nick, is the strong silent type when it comes to parenting. My mother is the one who's making the majority of the parenting decisions, and she's the only one trying to get me to stay in the school system in whatever way possible. And Wynn? My brother's simply wondering why we're always talking about Ty. *Why am I always the center of attention?*

The one and only thing that calms me down and makes me stop is drawing something or doing a visual puzzle. And even those little things, like making an illustration and seeing my mom praise me and put it on the fridge, are monumental, especially for an ADHD kid with no confidence like me. Nothing is getting through to me, yet this moment after seeing my mom shaken to the core blows my mind. I know I have problems I gotta get figured out.

My biological father, Gary, doesn't quite share my mother's patience or concern either. How can he, since he's nowhere to be found?

"ADAM RAISED A CAIN"

Demolition is all about tearing down and demolishing something. Sometimes I think I learn how to do this by following my fathers' examples in my life. They sure find a way to break down certain parts of me, whether by the things they say or do not say, depending on the father I'm talking about.

I think it's interesting when I hear someone say, "You must come from a strong family" or "Did your father teach you how to be a carpenter?" As if there is a parallel between a strong family and learning to be a skilled tradesman. Truth be known, I don't think I came from a strong family. As far as families go, the first model wasn't working well; in fact, my biological father doesn't work much at all. As I already shared, he's a talented musician who kind of has to live in the shadow of his more charismatic and more popular father, Big Daddy George Burton, the talented leader of a jazz group.

Big Daddy's son, Gary, has a lot of challenges ahead of him. I mean, all you've ever known as your office is a dark, smoky bar, and the libations are usually on the house. The workdays are mostly nights; therefore you kinda live gig to gig and paycheck to paycheck.

Gary has a lot of faults, but he's also clearly a lot of fun, at least from the endless stories I hear from his jazz buddies who visit my mom off and on through the years. It's only a matter of time—well, that and two kids—before my mom has to basically grab us and run. Because, after all, she's a cocktail waitress, going to college and trying to raise a family on tips. Let's just say my father wasn't providing much more than bad credit and debt. Oh yeah . . . and occasional random celebrations with money we don't have. So Mom takes my brother and me and splits.

It's safe to say my family isn't built on a strong foundation but rather contains lots of cracks and fault lines from the very beginning. And sometimes

when a foundation is crumbling, you need to be able to move that home to another location. It isn't easy, but it's often worth the trouble. Then again, you can just have some strangers arrive at your house, send you guys on vacation, and proceed to demolish the house. Mom chose the latter way to deal with Gary.

I do have a building story with Gary. When I'm fifteen years old, already getting rebellious, I decide to visit him over spring break. Wynn is a senior and heads down to Daytona to party and learn more about girls, so I find a way to get in touch with Gary through his sister, Gail. I want to know if the stories I've heard are real. I have to meet him at my aunt's house, since my mom would likely hunt him down if she knew he was in town.

When I finally meet my father, I'm wearing a London Taxi hat like I always did back then, and no joke, when my dad opens the door, he's wearing one too. It's surreal to see someone who resembles an older me have the same fashion sense. (Of course, I use the word *sense* very lightly.) My father drives me down to Ocoee, Florida, to introduce me to his new wife and their three daughters, and while driving, I study my father's hands. They look identical to mine. I notice the detail in them as he works the stick shift of his car; they're definitely the hands of a working man, not an artist but someone who spends a lot of time working with tools.

Wynn already has his opinion of my father at this time, and it's not the most favorable. Not long after our drive down to Florida, I see a glimpse of this firsthand when we stop at a gas station.

"Hey, Ty. You got five bucks I can borrow?"

I look at my father behind the wheel of the parked car and wonder if he's joking. I'm thinking, *Are you kidding? I'm fifteen. I mow lawns.* But I just nod and tell him sure and give him the $5. When he climbs back in the car a few minutes later, he's holding a can of beer.

"Don't say anything about this," Gary says.

When we get down to his home in Florida, I meet his wife, Paige, and their beautiful girls. That's one thing he can do—make attractive children. The girls are all really sweet and adorable. After I'm there for a while, he asks me what I'd like to do while I'm staying with them.

"Let's build something," I suggest.

"What do you want to build?"

"How 'bout a boat?"

So in the midst of Gary needing to find employment and actually sending out flyers to try to accomplish this, he spends time with me to construct a boat. We make it out of plywood, complete with a rudder and a sail on it. We end up polyurethaning it four times. For the first time in my life, someone's showing me how to do this and that, and he's my actual father. Doing the very thing fathers should do. It only takes fifteen years for it to happen.

Gary is good with his hands and can build things well. We spend a couple of days putting together this sturdy and attractive sailboat, and once we finish, we head to a lake to try it out. This is one of my all-time favorite stories. It's a truly incredible thing, going down to finally spend time with my dad, watching him show me how to build something with my own hands, and seeing it all come together so perfectly, a ship that can sail a whole new relationship. We get ready to launch it. We slip it into the water and watch as it begins to move steadily and then starts to sink and soon disappears. So . . . yeah. Perhaps this is a foreshadowing about our relationship. Someone's telling me, "Uh, yeah, Ty? That ship has literally already sailed, and just in case you're wondering, well, there you go."

I'm not finished with the "Dad and Demo" stories. So Gary's brother owns a construction company in Tampa. The first time I'm ever on a real construction site is when my father brings me over to let me work and earn a little money. My first job is pulling off the apron or skirt of the foundation frame (the wood you usually make a square mold out of). I'm prying off a large 2x12 when it pops off and shoots down toward my shins, making me jump back to avoid getting hit. I land on one of those large six-inch nails, puncturing the bottom of my foot. It feels great.

Needless to say, my uncle isn't so happy. His anger doesn't come out on me, however, but on his brother, Gary.

"Thanks so much, Gary, for bringing your child on the site! Now I have to take him to the hospital!"

For the first time, I realize what perception can do to a person. I can see how everybody looks down on my father, because basically everything he touches turns to a disaster. I feel bad because his own brother is wondering why he brought this estranged son who's never been on a construction site with him and now he's gotten himself injured.

When someone already sees you as a screwup, then you're doomed from the start. The great thing about my career after art school is nobody knew the first twenty years of my life, so they couldn't prejudge me when I came to them wanting work.

All I needed was one person—just one—to give me a chance.

"HERE COMES YOUR MAN"

Here's how one of my job interviews went. I go and put a poster board of my art on my potential employer's desk. The guy looks at the poster board covering half of his desk and glances back at me.

"What's this?" he asks.

"It's a piece I made in college."

"Okay. But I still don't understand. What do you do exactly?"

I nod and grin.

"I want to make logos."

"Sure, but this is *maybe* just the beginning of something, but there's no way I can hire you from seeing this."

This is when reality hits me. Yes, I only went to art school for one year, but I'm special. Everybody knows that. I was the most talented student in the class. And yeah, I know there were only seven students who ended up graduating, but still. I know I have the proper skills for this firm to hire me.

Turns out I'm not the guy for that design shop. After a few job interviews like this, I begin to have to face reality. I've gone from being praised in my class to suddenly thinking I'm absolutely unprepared for these meetings. I'm not even close to being ready to show off my work, because I don't have any real work to show.

When I end up landing an interview with one of the best firms in Atlanta, I decide to be creative. I take one of my Converse high tops, put wings on it, and paint it red, and then I send it to the company with a note that reads, "Just want to get a foot in the door." I know—very, very clever. When I meet with them, they tell me how much they appreciate my cleverness, yet they don't have a job for me.

"I'll work for free," I say.

"We don't need anybody now. Work on some logos and come back to us with a portfolio."

I'm getting that "you certainly seem to be creative" vibe from them.

The biggest challenge people have in life is to try to figure out what they're supposed to do with their lives. What am I good at? God knows we've all taken assessment tests that will end up stating the things that make us stand out and other nonsense like that. When I get out of art school, I know some of my strengths. Even though some of my heroes are artists like Picasso and Miró, I'm pretty sure I can't make money out of following their examples. I'm not going to set up outside a park and start to paint; I paint every day, but it just happens to be inside someone's home.

The heroes I'm trying to follow are the graphic designers I've studied. Super old-school like Woody Pirtle of Pentagram, whom I've already mentioned. Or the team that designed the Talking Heads album covers in the '80s. My heroes were in magazines like *Communication Arts*, *Graphic*, and *Archive*, journals geared toward ad campaigns as well as posters, business cards, album covers, etc. The reason a lot of these heroes don't have names is because, just like in furniture design, the artist or designers are hired to design under a company's brand, like Knoll or Herman Miller. And especially in Italy, young designers create amazing stuff but can't put their name on it until they make one for themselves and finally start their own company. It's the same in graphic design, so most of the guys I love are the ones behind the scenes.

I'm perfectly happy to be behind the scenes. But doing what? I have a commercial art technology degree, which basically means I can make things that are print-ready. Do you even remember this back in the day? So let me explain.

Back in the good ole 1980s, there are the things called mechanicals, where you have to paste every single image and word onto a board. This can involve stuff like cutting out Ruby film with an X-Acto knife and layering it onto a canvas and sketching out the images. You have to use a T-square and triangle in order for it to be precise and accurate. Then you're working with things like rubber cement and fonts that aren't coming on a computer screen but that you're cutting out. Once you put it on the board, it's there permanently unless you start over from scratch.

For a short while, I begin to work on mechanicals at *Georgia Trend* magazine. This is great since I have my foot in the door in the business, but that's only until a year later when a new machine is invented that makes me completely obsolete and useless.

"Yeah, there's this new thing called a Macintosh," someone tells me. "We actually don't need you to come in and make things print-ready anymore."

"But that's what I went to school for."

"Yeah. A lot of people are going to be out of work 'cause of it."

So you probably haven't heard of mechanicals, but I bet you've heard of Macintosh, right? I can't believe it.

I continue to work for *Georgia Trend*, basically coming in for four days at the end of each month to get the magazine ready to go to press. There's this hippie chick who works there who must like my skater style because one day we're talking, and she brings up an interesting job opportunity.

"There's a position for someone

who does mechanicals at a graphic design shop in Midtown that you might want to check out. I gave them your name."

Somewhere in the background, I think I hear "One Thing Leads to Another" by The Fixx.

When I arrive at Nancy Neil Design Studio, I discover the owner is a really sweet woman who runs the place along with a really funny copywriter.

"Do you know how to do mechanicals?" Nancy asks me.

I wonder if she knows about the Macintosh, but I'm not about to ask.

"Yeah. Definitely. I'm great with them."

Nancy hires me to do mechanicals, but what she doesn't realize is how I suck horribly at doing these. The key with making things print-ready is being precise, and I've never been good at being precise. Even in art school, my teacher would say, "Your ideas are amazing, but your complete mechanical and surgical execution is a bit atrocious." Well, thank you very much, but he was right. My T-bar has always been a little off. Frank Lloyd Wright, another idol of mine, would have fired me on the spot from any drafting table he'd see me at.

Thankfully, Nancy Neil has more mercy than most others. After I'm working for her for a week, the mechanicals begin to start stacking up because I'm taking three times as long to finish simply because I'm trying to get them right. Nancy eventually comes up to me with concern on her face.

"Ty, I really need these by the end of the day. They have to go out."

"I'm really trying," I say.

She sighs. "Give me the mechanicals. Here's what you can do. I need a logo for the Apparel Mart. They need it today. They need logos for the men's, women's, and children's wear. Just come up with some ideas."

This is huge. My boss of only a week is taking the grunt work and telling me to do something else, something a lot more creative and fun to do. In about ten minutes, I create a logo of a man, woman, and child that's basically just a graphic on which you can swap out the background pattern for whatever season it might be. When I show it to Nancy, I can tell she's impressed.

"So I can charge them three times for the same logo?" she asks.

"Actually, you can charge them nine times 'cause it's for three different logos."

Immediately she's like, *Okay, forget the mechanicals; here's your next project.*

This is one of those moments for me. A moment when someone gives you a chance to show off your creativity without knowing who you are, and you deliver right off the bat.

In the struggle with trying to figure out your place in the economic world and what you're good at, there are so many times you get rejected and told you're average. Time and time again, you hear, "It's okay but it's not great," and all the same lines of dismissal, but if you keep striving, there will eventually be that one moment—that one break of clarity—when someone believes in you. And the next thing you know, you shine.

After this validation, I started whipping out all sorts of projects for them. An art directors club had come up with a competition to do a uniquely themed party, so I came up with the idea for a theme based on the movie *Psycho* that ended up winning an award. The invitation had Norman Bates on the cover and had a shower cap inside it. The party had fun little prizes like "Best Use of Shower Cap" and other silly things like that.

I go from doing a terrible job at mechanicals to helping the firm win an award. Talk about awesome. I end up working with Nancy for two and a half years.

I can't say enough about Nancy Neil. For the first time in my life, someone comes along and basically says, "I'm going to help you because you need help." Up to that point, I haven't seen a lot of that in my life. I learn later on that when Nancy was in college, some anonymous person randomly paid for her tuition. She never knew who it was, but ever since then, something was planted in her heart to help the underdog.

Lucky Ty Pennington, some might say. But here's a great snapshot of my life back then. Yes, I'm very lucky, but I'll say this over and over again: the pendulum swings both ways. Here's a great example.

While working for Nancy, I find this really beautiful 1972 Volkswagen with a two-tone interior. I save $600 and borrow another $600 from Nancy to buy it. I'm so excited that I rush to the office so all my coworkers can see it. I park it behind the building and leave it running while I quickly drop in and tell everybody to come and check out my VW. When I get back outside, the car is gone. Someone had stolen it. I'm screaming "No!!!" all while my coworkers are shaking their heads and saying, "You left it running? Who does that?"

That's a great snapshot of my life. (A stolen snapshot.)

Another great snapshot? Getting an invitation from a stranger to go to Japan.

Who does that?

Pennington. Ty Pennington.

"BIG IN JAPAN"

Let's get back to destruction.

I'm not exactly sure why I've always been so drawn toward demolishing almost anything. No, really—anything . . . I don't discriminate. If it's a bicycle, dishwasher, sofa, Ming vase, screen door, television, toys, I don't care. In fact, the first gift my stepfather ever gives me is a cool, clear plastic truck. I'm mesmerized by its design because you actually can see the colorful gears turning inside the mechanism. Some gears are larger and extend to the outside so they can be used to wind up the truck for speed. Of course, within minutes I'm not only wound up myself but also bleeding profusely all over the new toy after having fallen chin-first right on top of the biggest and sharpest gear. So yeah. I've also always been really great at demolishing myself as well.

"Accident-prone" is what they call it. Talk about a gift; this is mine. Unfortunately, this is also the last sharp object I'll ever have given to me as a gift. I mean, I kind of understand: one minute I'm elated and laughing, the next, BAM, I'm spewing blood all over the floor and the furniture. So yeah, even gifts are things I can destroy pretty well, not to mention jobs and relationships.

This gift of demolishing things really makes me feel SPECIAL. Like when my parents see me jumping over kids lying down under a ramp and me volunteering to do the same, of course while never wearing a helmet. No wonder they cringe when I'm finally old enough to mow the lawn.

Thinking back now, I realize this may be the reason I read so many comic books. (I prefer the phrase *graphic novels*.) The stories are about mutants with special powers. And what are they great at? They all have unique abilities to demolish anything and everything they touch. These mutant powers vary quite a bit. Some have bones and claws made of titanium, while others can freeze or burn any object they desire. Some even have cool powers called the Power Cosmic encompassing all things . . . Oh so deep, that Silver Surfer. But I think my favorite is the power of Havok, the youngest brother of a family of mutants with power to absorb and harness any cosmic energy. I love Havok because he is forced to move to the desert alone until he can learn to control his powers. Basically, the guy can blow up or implode anything when pushed too far, which usually is done by his older brother. (Awwww, family. Brotherly love is the best.)

Truth be told, my brother and I are both obsessed with these mutants with superpowers. We not only collect the comics, but we race home after school to watch one of our favorite shows called *Ultraman*. This guy has some social and identity issues, never really saying anything but possessing a keen ability to throw random karate chops in the air. (Sort of like the kid who squares off and says, "You want a piece of this? I know karate and jujitsu too!" after chopping and kicking at nothing but air.)

Ultraman has these cool lasers that shoot out of his hands and maybe even his eyes. It's hard to tell if he even has eyes since he's always wearing a silver mask to match his silver skin and tights. Come to think of it, he looks like a Japanese version of the Tin Man from *The Wizard of Oz*, except Ultraman has this red light that starts to blink when he's running out of power. This happens a lot since he spends most days fighting gigantic monsters like Godzilla.

This street fighting is quite destructive; in fact, these guys do more destruction and damage to the buildings in Tokyo (aka the miniature model set in a studio) than they do to each other. Seriously, it's like this: chop swing, miss, hit building, demolish homes; then Godzilla counters by swinging his tail, which again misses and demolishes homes and buildings. All while frightened police squads wearing motorcycle helmets (for safety, I guess) yell at each other between trying to communicate with Ultraman, who is clearly distracted and busy wrestling an enormous lizard off his meds.

No wonder my brother and I are glued to the TV set. I certainly can relate to missing the mark this consistently, not to mention demolishing everything I ever touch. I like to think my fashion sense is a little better, but back then in the '70s, whoooh. It's hard to say.

So hold on. Don't leave and skip to the next chapter—not yet. There's a point to this story, and it involves how I become a model.

It's 1986, and I'm working for Nancy Neil. One day while I'm on the street skateboarding, I'm approached by a stranger who tells me I should be a model.

"I know how you can make a lot of money," the guy tells me.

I nod. "Uh-huh. I'm sure you can. I'm just not really ready for that type of work."

Undaunted, the man gives me his card and tells me to mention his name at the agency. I hold his card and realize he must be legit. I'm like, *Wow, this is serendipitous*, because the company he works for is called—wait for it—Serendipity.

I'm sporting a rattail so it's not like I'm expecting someone to start taking photos of me. When I go down to the agency the man sends me to, I tell them exactly what he told me.

"This guy, Mark, told me to come in. Thought I might be able to do some modeling work and make some money to pay for school."

I get a bunch of blank stares.

"Who told you that?"

"Mark."

"We don't know who you're talking about."

So I hand them the card he gave me.

"Yeah, we still have no idea who you're talking about," they say.

I assume they're lying to me.

"Have you ever had photos made?" someone asks.

"No."

"Any experience?"

"No."

"Well, why don't you have some photographs made and come back."

"Well," I reply, "that's sorta what I assumed you guys would do here."

During this whole conversation that's going nowhere, there's a Japanese guy in the office pointing over at me and laughing. It becomes so obvious that I ask the guys I'm talking with what this guy's problem is.

"Oh, don't worry. He's a Japanese scout from Japan. Picking out models. He must like you."

Maybe it's my childhood appreciation for Japanese mutant action shows like *Ultraman*. Or maybe it's the line of menswear clothing I'm sporting, which consists of a thrift store suit jacket, hand-painted in Jackson Pollock style of 1980 splatter, decorated with metal safety pins on the lapel and collars. Whatever it is, the talent scout from Japan walks over to me as I'm trying to explain to the woman at Serendipity that, yes, Mark did actually send me. All she can say is, "Who said you could be a model?" and "Do you have any pictures without the rattail? I mean, have you seen yourself?" This Godzilla, God bless her, isn't a fan of my look, but when I ask the woman why this guy is laughing at me, she tells me he thinks I should go to Japan.

"Why?" I ask the talent scout.

"Because you make lots of money."

So naturally I'm like, "Well, shishito! When do we leave?"

Thus begins the slow building of pictures, confidence, culture, architecture, and artistic creative consumption, followed by the inevitable demolition of my dislocated shoulder (skateboarding/Vespa scooter riding accident) all while still keeping my other job as a graphic designer. I don't know a thing about fashion or modeling, but I do know an opportunity when I see one. I also know change is almost always good, and going somewhere you've never been is without question always the right thing to do. Even if it means being away from what you've always known as home for more than four months.

When I show my contract to my stepdad, who is studying to be a lawyer, he warns me about making any rash decisions.

"This basically says you're going into child slavery," he says. "You're only guaranteed $2,000 for your entire trip. You have to pay for your apartment, meals, everything. And you can't leave until you pay off everything. You could be there for a long time!"

"I don't care! Never been. Gonna go."

There's no way I'm not going. Sure, I have no idea where I'm going, but when does something like this ever happen to you, where someone comes along and says, "I'm going to pay for you to go to Tokyo"? There's no way to begin to understand what a crazy, busy, and bustling city really looks like. But sometimes one ticket to a new destination can change your direction and dedication for life. Tokyo is literally the center of the universe in 1986. Everything is designed or built, or, let's face it, made even smarter and smaller in this city, yet my knowledge and my portfolio will only become bigger if I go.

Unfortunately, I never make a lot of money as the Ultraman scout suggests. In fact, I'm sent home after my arm keeps popping out of the socket, and after the fourth time, someone has to put their foot in my armpit and pull my arm until it finally snaps back into place. They decide I'm fun but not financially viable. So I may not have made a stack of yen, but I do make friends with cool humans. Skaters. Artists. Photographers. Musicians. Models. Sumo wrestlers. Well . . . you get the idea. Japan not only opens a door of opportunity; it opens my mind to what a fast-paced, kinetic, and energetic metropolis looks like. It's not for everyone, but it certainly fits a mutant whose power is chaos. Tokyo is definitely magical for me, and once you have a taste of something more—well, you want . . . more.

So my life lesson? In life, random doors will show up in front of you. DO NOT RUN THE OTHER WAY. No matter what happens.

"MAMA SAID KNOCK YOU OUT"

"To me, making a tape is like writing a letter—there's a lot of erasing and rethinking and starting again . . . A good compilation tape, like breaking up, is hard to do."*

That's a fabulous line from Nick Hornby's great novel *High Fidelity*, which they turned into a fabulous movie as well. You remember mixtapes, right? At least you probably do if you were born before 2000. Cassettes are what we used to play back in the day before everybody began to buy compact discs and long before iPods and digital music became the thing. Wait, are iPods even around any-

more? In a lot of ways, my entire life has been one gigantic mixtape, where I'm changing songs and recording a new one over an older one, and where I rewind and then fast-forward and then accidentally erase my entire B side. In

---

* Nick Hornby, *High Fidelity* (New York: Riverhead, 1995), 88–89.

1991, I kind of do just that, inadvertently falling into an entirely new direction in my career. And I literally mean falling.

The year 1991 is a groundbreaking one for music, when grunge decides to sucker punch the hair bands and synth-pop of the '80s and go in a whole new direction. Which is ironic because that's sorta what's going to happen in my life too. I'll sum up how everything suddenly and drastically changes by creating for you an imaginary mixtape:

1. "SMELLS LIKE TEEN SPIRIT" BY NIRVANA. It's maybe the quintessential grunge song, the anthem for Generation X. This song is released that year, and the title is ironic since I'm twenty-seven years old but still look like a teenager. So far this is helping me continue to get modeling work. I'm not making any money but I'm having fun and I keep adding photos to my book.

I book a gig for half a day for a J.Crew catalog and earn $500, which after the agency's commission is down to $400. I don't think much of the shoot. They take a bunch of photos of me and other guys in our swim trunks, and I'm really just another dude in the background. I'm living down in Miami earning money driving RVs while occasionally modeling. The most exciting thing for me about this shoot is that they're using my cool, old Chevy Nova wagon as a prop.

2. "I'M TOO SEXY" BY RIGHT SAID FRED. Yeah, so I'm feeling too sexy when I'm told they're putting me on the cover of the J.Crew catalog. The photo is me sitting there with a razor. All these other models are like, "Dude! You got the [insert colorful language here] cover!" I'm like, "There's no way. I *didn't* get it." I remember this moment. It's one of those "moments."

So far I've been struggling in modeling. Sure, I've been lucky enough to travel a little bit and see the world, but I've never gotten a big gig or campaign. I'm making no money. But the moment I see the catalog cover, I know everything's going to change.

Get ready, Ty. The phone's going to be ringing off the hook.

This song is also foreshadowing, since Right Said Fred is a one-hit wonder . . .

3. "SUMMERTIME" BY DJ JAZZY JEFF AND THE FRESH PRINCE. It's the summer of 1991, and around the same time I make the J.Crew cover, I happen to be going through a tough time. I've broken up with a serious girlfriend and realize that I just need to get away from everything. Along with a buddy of mine named William, I decide to drive across the country to California, carrying a JVC camcorder for documenting our adventures. William and I are in a band called "Thick and Vainy"; he's the thick, while (no surprise here) I'm the vain one.

4. "GOOD VIBRATIONS" BY MARKY MARK AND THE FUNKY BUNCH. This sums up the mood and gives you a picture of a good-looking guy without his shirt on

Tygert

Height 180 Chest 96 Waist 79 Hips 96 Shoes 26.5 Hair Brown Eyes Green

riding in a Jeep heading to the West Coast. "Feel it. Feel it. Feel the vibration." All the waiting around for calls and being told "We're going in another direction" and making $20 for half a day's worth of work are all finally paying off. I'm finally entering the next stage of whatever's next for Ty. Life is good.

Also, just so you know, the only reason I throw in Marky Mark is because he uses a sample of Lou Reed's "Walk on the Wild Side" on one of his jams. And The Velvet Underground are pretty close to the greatest of all time.

5. "UNBELIEVABLE" BY EMF. For a while, that's how I'm feeling. (And by the way, this song ends up becoming the soundtrack to *Extreme* a decade later.) Picture me crawling out onto the hood of the Jeep with my big JVC camera and filming the road moving at a high speed. I'm wearing goggles and lean over the camera so you can see my head enter the screen. The incredible Butthole Surfers are wailing through the speakers while we speed through the mountains and canyons of West Texas and New Mexico. If any accident is going to happen, this is the place, but no, we've safely gone four days wheeling through Big Ben cranking Led Zeppelin's "Gallows Pole" and "Achilles Last Stand."

Maybe it's William choosing to drive on my day to get behind the wheel, or maybe it's the music we're listening to after touring the caves in Carlsbad Caverns that evening while setting off toward the western sunset. We're listening through double headphones to our own horrible music, and this somehow makes us drowsy, which is surprising, which is a fabulous way to introduce our next song.

6. "ENTER SANDMAN" BY METALLICA. Uh-oh. Something bad is about to happen. So we're driving in Santa Rosa, New Mexico, literally two days from California. William slides off onto the soft shoulder, realizes it, and tries to quickly get back on the razor-sharp highway, but the Jeep flips! Five or six times. Of course, we're not wearing seat belts, so we're tossed out onto the coral reef road. The good thing is William and I are still alive, but . . . Wait, that's another song.

7. "ALIVE" BY PEARL JAM. The crazy thing is that after coming to consciousness, I stare down at my now naked body but see no bleeding. Strangers are trying to wrap us in blankets. That's when I realize my entire backside—yes, backside—is ripped away, leaving gravel and road particles buried in my skin. I think the roll bar landed on my thighs but somehow bounced over me, because standing is difficult.

Inside the ambulance, they place us in suspended straps since we can't lie on our backs. I suddenly recall the moments after the accident, with the Jeep sitting in the middle of the road behind William and me.

"Where's the Jeep?" he asks, just before it explodes and gets his attention. No joke. It's like some action movie gone horribly wrong.

Amazingly, I don't break a single bone in the accident, but I lose a massive amount of skin. The nurses have to scrub our wounds with steel wool to get the rocks and debris out—seriously it's the most intense pain

I've ever experienced. However, we're given morphine and Jell-O to ease the pain.

I never seem to do anything medium . . . it's always maximum.

Oh yeah. The next day I have a talk with myself, and it's quite the conversation. Just like how I left the flipping Jeep, I literally seem to leave my body. I find myself near the ceiling, looking down at myself and just shaking my head.

Wow, Ty. You look really stupid when you mumble.

Clearly the morphine is getting me higher than I've ever been. But after that I've never stopped talking to myself, because at this moment I realize that maybe I sometimes actually listen.

Oh, and one other thing. This is the last time I ever see my young Kardashian bottom. The next day while trying to walk with my IV, my skin—aka rear end—well, it literally slides off with my pus-covered bandages and hits the floor. After that it's been as flat as the desert plains. Sometimes you've got to leave your behind in the past.

⑧."MORE THAN WORDS" BY EXTREME. I don't know about this song, but the next moment that comes to mind is definitely extreme—and I don't quite have the words to describe it. I end up heading back to Atlanta to heal, and I end up staying with my ex-girlfriend and her boyfriend. Really, imagine the scene, interrupting their making-out session while I'm calling out from the bathroom, "Hey, guys, would you mind soaking me in the bath again?"

Then her new boyfriend's just shaking his head. "Dude, really? You have to almost kill yourself to try to get her back?"

"That's what love is," I tell him.

9. "WHERE IS MY MIND?" BY THE PIXIES. (Yes, this song is from 1988, but really, it's timeless and from an amazing band. So there.) When I get back to Miami, I continue to make money driving RVs around, but now some calls start coming in. I book a job for Swatch, the Swiss watch company. I figure it will be easy. All I'll have to do is put a hat and a shirt on and just show my wrist. No problem. When I arrive at the shoot, my stomach instantly drops. These Italian guys are directing the photo shoot with all these people splashing around in a pool.

This isn't going to be pretty.

I take off my shirt, knowing I literally have staples still in my head, with a whole area of my hair shaved. Parts of my shoulders and back look like they've been used to sand down a table. The Italian guys call up my agency and yell at them. "Who is this guy you sent us? Frankenstein? What were you thinking?"

There's my mind—"way out in the water, see it swimmin'"!

10. "IT AIN'T OVER 'TIL IT'S OVER" BY LENNY KRAVITZ. Yes, Lenny, it ain't over. Not just yet. I need my brother, Wynn, to put the final touch on this episode of *Extreme Makeover: Ty Edition.*

After recognizing that maybe the beaches of Miami aren't the best place to pick up modeling gigs anymore in my present condition, I drive back to Atlanta, taking my modeling portfolio full of all the photographs I've had taken of me over the years. Remember, this is 1991, so not only do we not have digital music, but we also don't have digital photos we can keep in the cloud.

11. "GIVE IT AWAY" BY RED HOT CHILI PEPPERS. See where this is heading? One night when I'm spending the night at a friend's house, I remember that my modeling book is in Wynn's car, so I call him to make sure he takes all my bags into his apartment. He's not living in the best area in Atlanta. Okay, I'll be honest—he lives in the ghetto. Sure enough, Wynn parks his car on the street and either forgets to get my

bags or doesn't care, so someone breaks into his car and takes my portfolio. When I realize it's gone, I can't believe it.

"Wynn, you've single-handedly ended my fashion career."

"Oh yeah?" my brother says. "If the pictures were so important, why'd you leave them in my car?"

"Because you said you were going to take them inside!"

So not only have I been scarred after a serious wreck, but now I've lost my book with any proof that I ever had any pics. Yeah, sure, some people will remember the J.Crew ad, but most everything else is gone.

"Did you back up your book?" people will ask me.

Do they know me? I can't even remember to pay my electricity bill.

(12.)"MAMA SAID KNOCK YOU OUT" BY LL COOL J. Here's the beauty of life. After getting into the accident and becoming unable to model, and then losing the only proof I was a model in the first place, I'm forced to have to come to terms with my situation.

Okay, so that phase of my life is done. I need to go back to doing construction and refinishing furniture and other things I'm good at.

A year later, I'll get a casting call for doing something I'm really good at. But the only way that happens is when I move to Atlanta and start building things again and I become known for being good at those sorts of things.

This is like the stream hitting that rock. The modeling ends for some reason.

Was it someone saying to me, "You gotta stop doing this, Ty"? Who knows. All I know is, "Dude, you don't have a book anymore." I probably would not have ever stopped the modeling journey if it didn't end with such a definitive finality. I had reached a peak with the cover and believed I could be in the industry for another ten years. Life would have been very different.

After you hit a wall like that (or in my case, when you're in a Jeep tumbling down a hill), instead of being sad and depressed about things, you need to stand up and be ready for another opportunity to show itself. Figure out the things you love to do and keep doing them. In my case, it's creating pieces of furniture, building things, and revamping old houses, which leads to a job I'm relatively good at.

You can't see the future coming; God knows I get in my own way so many times. That's our biggest struggle in life—when you get in the way of yourself!

Day

13/16"

1-5/8"   1-5/8"

13/16"

FOUNDATION

Foundation

"UNCONTROLLABLE URGE"

Before you build a house, you have to lay a foundation. That foundation must be strong enough to hold up the weight of the house, and it also plays a role in *shaping* the house. Some foundations are built into the bedrock to give it extra support; some are not.

I think the foundation of your personality is also what shapes you early on in your life. One might call it your own personal footprint on which your life is built. This foundation may be the first step to your future, and like a house, it's drying out over time, but it's never really truly "cured" until, well, after the framing and finishing are done.

Actually, come to think of it, the foundation of my life was a layering of concrete efforts too, all meant to eradicate strains, stains, fractures, and reoccurring leaks. None of which would ever seem to CURE. However, they did somehow make me stronger. You know what they say: "What doesn't kill you only makes you . . ." Well, in my case, it's often "wronger." Yes, I know that's not a word. But sometimes it's hard to find the right word to summarize the moments that mold and sometimes shatter the strong person that will undoubtedly be the future you.

Let me tell you about one "hard to find the words for" moment when I was eight years old. It was the first moment I remember seeing a bus move in front of me. *Unforgettable* is too gentle of a word. *Excitement* is another word that just doesn't really seem to cover it. Although, surprisingly enough, covering is exactly what I was trying to do.

Imagine the sound of a bus switching gears, followed by its brakes squeaking a little as they lunge forward. Now imagine all the hardworking people sitting inside also lunging forward to witness quite a rare sight out their windows. Their faces seem shocked and full of surprise. Meanwhile, from outside the bus, I see looks of confusion and horror creep onto their gasping expressions through the windows. These folks are mainly impoverished African American women who work days and nights to support their families. This may be the reason they stare so intently at my wailing face. After all, it's not every day they pass an eight-year-old white kid crying at a bus stop as he holds his soiled underwear over his head almost like a trophy he's received. But this is no trophy; it's more like a form of water torture, or maybe that scene from *Unbroken* where the Olympics runner-turned-prisoner lifts the huge beam over his head for hours, overcome by pain and agony. Yeah. That's more of the feeling.

This was a cruel punishment inflicted on me by my hilarious babysitter and neighbor, who had a wicked, dark sense of humor. The object of this lesson—we'll just call it the "Dirty Bottom Bus Stop Photobomb Lesson" (sadly, before there are cameras or phones handy)—is to embarrass me so "extremely" that I'm CURED of wetting the bed. Like a showerhead that never stops leaking, this is a habit I was unable to break, until, well, I finally did.

Actually, everyone who's part of that moment breaks something. The bus driver breaks into hysterical laughter, along with my babysitter, my brother, and the neighbor kids hiding behind the trees. A pregnant lady on the bus possibly breaks her water, laughing so hard she spits up. My parents break out a bottle of wine after hearing of the news once they return that evening. And, of course, I not only break into tears, but I also break the habit of ever wetting myself. (Okay . . . well, there are a few couches and futons that are also broken during my college years, but that's a story for another time.)

My point is that this is a moment that not only breaks me but also begins to fix me too. It also makes for great book titles, such as *Build a Better You, One Brief at a Time*, *The Brief Case: For Better or Worse*, and *A Brief History of Time*. Anyway, this early foundation building is now something I will remember forever, especially when I look back and think about how far I've come.

Fast-forward a few decades to when I'm holding a dipped-in-gold Emmy Award over my head as an entire ballroom cheers when *Extreme Makeover: Home Edition* wins "Outstanding Reality Series" for changing people's lives. Priceless. Not to mention, the incredible moment when THAT bus moves and tears really do start to fly. Now that's a much more pleasant visual. Seeing those faces full of shock and awe—that's the type of indescribable moment that can CURE you of almost any unpleasant memory involving moving buses.

why start 1 project when you can almost finish 3?

"TIME"

Two chapters on my book finished, five more to go. Days or chapters? I don't know. All work and no play make Ty a tame boy. I feel like that great Pink Floyd song: "And you run and you run to catch up with the sun, but it's sinking." That's what happens when there's not enough hours in the day.

Welcome to my life.

So true story: I was opening a store in Venice, California, a few years back called "ADHD," short for "Art*Design*Home*Décor." Good name, right? I was so busy building and designing rooms and houses across America that my store was taking a bit longer to have the grand opening. So I eventually wrote a message in the glass window display:

> ADHD. Why start one project when you can almost finish 3?

"GET UP, STAND UP"

Going extreme is sometimes easier said than done.

The whole idea of thinking and doing things to the extreme is what we're all drawn to. Bigger is better, but the bigger the project, well ... the bigger the problems. Okay, we're getting ahead of ourselves, which is kind of exactly what happens.

Let me start over.

After the first pilot episode of *Extreme*, we don't deliver the show they originally pitched or cast all these different personalities for. However, we all know we have something special that's never been done before. We did a makeover on not just one room but all the rooms plus the exterior, not to mention a giant pirate ship with a slide going into the pool. For the first episode, we change the life of a struggling family and go pretty EXTREME with the makeover. These are all groundbreaking events that leave us in tears, for many reasons. It's emotionally draining, not to mention physically exhausting.

Once you have a taste of doing something that's never been done, such as rebuilding a house in seven insane days, you want a few days to sleep it off, but then you want to go even further, to push life to the extreme. The other problem with actually pulling off the impossible is that you think you can do it again, only slightly better. And bigger. It makes sense, right? Logic tells us that if you did it once, then you can do it again. But some things, like building a house in fewer days than the fingers on your hands, aren't exactly logical. Or sane, for that matter.

It's one thing to accomplish greatness with the same team of workers who learn from being in the trenches for the first time; it's another when you're renovating houses for the first time on the first show to ever do this, working with a different builder *each time.* Meaning it's a new experience for a rookie contractor, yet we're trying to go even bigger than what we did last time.

Think about that. Let's say you're a builder, and you hear about a show that's doing incredible things by helping deserving families. So you say to yourself, *You know what? I think me and my crew of subs want to build the next one with you guys.* After phone calls with the previous builder, explaining what to look out for and how to stay on schedule (as if that's even humanly possible), you tell yourself you can do it—simply because it's such a rush going into the unknown. To climb a mountain you've never climbed. We have all these good-hearted people, with sleeves rolled up and tools in their hands, not to mention our crew and design team. Then there's me, leading all of us with a megaphone in hand into this cloud of uncertainty.

Fortunately, we also have the power of editing what's seen on television. Because, whooooo . . . talk about the agony of defeat. We have some of the most extreme disasters ever once the demolition is complete and we begin the first and very excruciating phase of the rebuilding.

Even if demolition goes well, the real test comes the minutes or hours it takes to pour the foundation. If that takes too long, then the framing crew will be waiting for hours, and these aren't the hours when people wait long. When it's 2:00 or 3:00 a.m. before the foundation is ready to frame, those guys who've been waiting since 8:00 p.m. are gonna bolt. Who can blame them? They have families, as well as other jobs, they have to get back to.

So now you can see how it starts. Just one delay causes a ripple effect all the way down the line. Trying to get a framing crew together at 3:00 a.m.? A little difficult. You'll hear lots of "leave a message, and I'll get back to you" recordings. Yeah. If you're lucky. And when you're going *Extreme,* luck swings both ways. Now that you're delayed, the electric, plumbing, and drywall crews are being pushed back, or just deciding to take rain checks. The general contractor has been up for two or three days without sleep and is starting to implode. Of course, with all these deteriorating delays and drama, my job is to go find the guy and ask him how it's going.

"It looks like we're a little behind. How are you feeling about all this?"

The poor guy's voice is already gone, but he wants to believe it when he tells me, "We're a little behind, but we'll make it up." Let me tell you something. I've learned over time that you *never* make it up. It actually feels like time speeds up as you get older. And that's exactly how our general contractor looks—like he's aged twenty years in three days. Just like time, Murphy's Law is waiting around every corner. You can't see it coming, but when it hits, it hits hard. That law is swift and harsh. "Anything that can go wrong will go wrong."

Eventually we get so behind that our GC collapses just after mumbling, apologizing, and possibly crying. No joke. I feel so bad for this guy. He's climbing Everest for the first time without

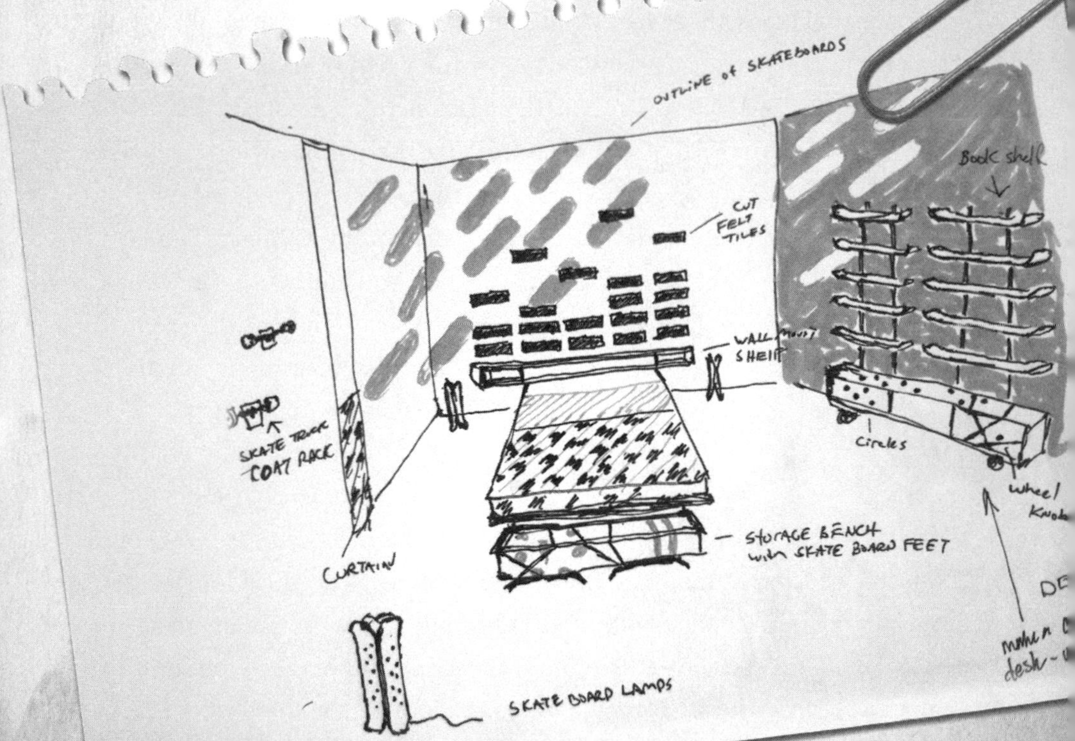

OUTLINE of SKATEBOARDS

CUT FELT TILES

Book shelf

WALL MOUNT SHELF

SKATE TRUCK COAT RACK

Circles

wheel knob

STORAGE BENCH with SKATE BOARD FEET

CURTAIN

SKATE BOARD LAMPS

DE
mohen
desk

realizing he is barely breathing oxygen. I've always admired that "never quit" spirit, and he never does. But it literally almost kills him. As we watch the Sherpas carry him down the mountain of stacked lumber still waiting to go up, we realize this "building to the extreme" is a wonderful high when it goes well, but a horrible low when it doesn't.

Now with more volunteers and workers standing around looking for answers to what we should do, we call for backup. It's 911—we call every contractor we know who can come help save the day. Luckily about four different ones with crews show up. Literally an hour later. I'll never forget how humble our exhausted GC is when he thanks the new teams for showing up.

"Look, guys, I don't know all of you, but I got in over my head and needed help. Thank you from the bottom of my heart for leaving your jobs and families to be here. Let's build this house—together."

Sometimes the real hero is the one who knows his limitations and sees the benefit of working as a team. That and the benefit of getting a short nap. I think those really tough moments of feeling like you're failing when everyone's expecting something great can cause you to lose confidence in yourself. But then someone shows up in your life and says, "You look like you could use some help." This right here is the magical spirit of what being a part of *Extreme* is all about.

In this moment, we turn our hard hats around backward. I channel my best *Braveheart* speech while screaming into my megaphone, "Let's do this!" and leading the charge. Sure enough, within forty-eight hours, we make up an entire lost day. It makes us push the reveal by one day, but we reach the summit.

I guess it's true what they say about the struggle: the harder it is to

> Sometimes the real hero is the one who knows his limitations and sees the benefit of working as a team.

achieve, the sweeter the feeling of overcoming it. And being overcome with feeling is exactly what happens to us once the family sees not only the bus move but their lives move in a new and more positive direction. Which, come to think of it, is how we all feel. Well, that and needing to take a really long shower.

So to sum it up. Going big is extremely amazing. There's never the option of walking away. Only running toward it, or toward something even bigger the next time. As I just said, the harder it is to achieve something, the sweeter the feeling you have when you overcome it.

Just when you've reached your lowest point, that's when you go back to your beginnings, your fundamentals. When you draw on all the hard-knock lessons and experiences you have. Sometimes for me, I think of the loving and patient wisdom a father might share with his son, and then I imagine what it might have been like if I'd ever had any of that.

The harder it is to achieve something, the sweeter the feeling you have when you overcome it.

"ANOTHER BRICK IN THE WALL (PART 2)"

When you're laying a foundation, you start using a word like *PSI*, which means "pounds per square inch." This is how you measure the amount of pressure that can be put on the foundation. One of the questions I always get asked about *Extreme* is "How can you get the foundations to cure fast enough to build houses on top of them?" Usually a slab takes a month or a few weeks to cure.

The answer? We'd use a *hot mix* because it cures rapidly. Which is the opposite of my situation as a kid because I was a *hot mess*. I put a lot of pressure on my foundation. They didn't seem to be able to find a cure at all. In fact, there is still no cure. There's just, let's call it, an *additive* that seems to help.

My stepfather was definitely the additive in my foundation. I had plenty of problems while I was still curing as a crazy child.

Nick Pennington is everything we aren't in my family. Quiet, intelligent, and someone who had a free ride—a scholarship—to college. Nick is also a super-talented bass player who once took a bus from Sarasota, Florida to New York City with his best friend when he was only fifteen years old. They snuck into the back of a jazz club and saw Coltrane live. That changed his life. Well, so did falling madly in love with my mom, even after meeting her loud and obnoxious boys and being friends with her ex. And speaking of foundation, Nick sure had a firm one, having a strong military father who believed children should be seen and not heard, a philosophy, as I've already said, that Nick adopted as well.

There's a story about my stepdad that my mom tells me. It takes place on the military base playground. Wynn and I aren't the nicest boys while on the playground, and there's one kid I think I'm treating horribly. I'd tell him, "I'm playing with your toy. It's mine now." And "you're going to do what I want to do," and nonsense like that. Just like little brats can do. Well, this kid probably gets sick of hearing my voice, so one day he has enough, and he begins to punch me in the face.

My stepdad's been watching my behavior on the playground from his office window, so he knows what's been happening. When the kid finally decides to whale on me, my stepdad calls my mom over to watch.

"Somehow this brings such joy to me," he says.

That's my stepdad. He always looked at me as if he knew something was coming but I didn't see it quite yet. At this point in my life, I'm blind to the reality of life with ADHD—heck, all of us were—so my whole mantra is to create chaos and have fun, all while my stepfather just seems to be thinking, *You have no idea what's coming for you, Ty.*

My stepdad says a very important thing to me when I'm young. Obviously he's not like my mom; he's not quite as patient when it comes to my behavior. But with or without ADHD, let's face it, I'm always trying to use my cuteness to get anything I can get away with. One day, I'm going off on a tangent, thinking I'm being amusing and adorable and making a show for my family, but my stepdad isn't finding it amusing at all. He's trying to explain something to me, yet all I keep saying is, "I know, I know." After a dozen times, he leans down and looks me in the eyes.

"Ty, let me tell you something. If you keep saying, 'I know' like that, like you think you know what you're talking about and you don't, and if you keep acting like you're so adorable—and sure, you're young and you have your great looks . . . But here's what's going to happen: when you're older, you're not going to have those. All you're going to have is what you know, and right now, you don't know a thing. And people will realize this—that you don't know crap."

My stepdad has this way of scaring you with reality. I guess that's the difference between a father figure and mother figure.

"Honey, don't do that," Mom will say. "You're going to end up a homeless man without two teeth because you think your good looks are going to get you through life. But you know what? They won't."

This is one of those moments in my life when someone's telling me to shut up and stop. The difficult thing for my stepdad is that I'm not his flesh and blood. So many times during my childhood, I could see him looking at my mom and thinking, *This loud child came from you?* He wants to discipline me but can't really lay a hand on me. But he can certainly give me stern lectures and emotional smackdowns.

My stepfather is right when he tells me this. I won't always be able to rely on my cute charm to get me through life. By the time I turn thirty, I realize there's not a lot of things I can rely on. I can finally see what my stepdad could see. It hits and hits me hard.

"ROAD TO NOWHERE"

There's one definition of foundation I found that's perfect for this chapter: "The lowest division of a building, wall, or the like, usually of masonry and partly or wholly below the surface of the ground."

Lowest . . . below the surface . . . Yeah, that pretty much sums up where I'm at in 1995. Let me set the stage, or the foundation, for you.

I'm around thirty years old and doing a lot of traveling back and forth between California and Atlanta, having followed a girlfriend out to the Golden State and finding work with the art department on *Leaving Las Vegas*. And by the way, it's always cool to forever be able to IMDB myself and see a movie pop up that garnered all kinds of awards, including earning Nicolas Cage an Oscar. In the meantime, I barely have any cash and am looking for any way to make some. So my brother comes to me with an idea and an opportunity.

"We need to buy this warehouse," Wynn tells me.

We visit the two-story building in Castlebury Hill, one of the oldest neighborhoods in Atlanta. Also known as "Snake Nation," the area is notorious in its early days as being on the wrong side of the tracks, with tunnels dug underneath and where you could find liquor and ladies of the night during the prohibition movement. Now, of course, it's an artist community just steps from the football/soccer stadium, the Georgia Aquarium, and Centennial Park. Wynn is really one of the first pioneers to move in back in the late 1980s. He's still there today.

When I enter the warehouse for the first time, I'm surprised to see the five hundred pianos sitting in the dark, gathering dust and in dire need of repair.

"What are we going to do?" I ask my brother. "Shoot an Elton John video?"

The guy who owns the building runs a company where he repairs and fixes up pianos, but since there are holes in the roof, all these pianos are getting ruined. If we purchase the building, we'll have a year to fix up the place before we have to start paying the mortgage, giving us equity to create some apartments to earn some income on. Since we have to come up with a down payment of around $32,000, Wynn and I partner with two other guys so we each have to come up with $8,000. We agree that if we buy the warehouse, we'll all put in time and labor to fix it up. When we actually have to write out checks, I'm about thirty cents short, so I ask the other guys to cover the rest, promising them I'll make it up to them and fix up the warehouse.

Here's the truth about renovating warehouses: everything is warped and nothing is straight. Just imagine trying to sand a floor that looks like elephants have stampeded over it.

Since I'm still in California working on films, my brother and the other guys start to get irked that I'm not doing my part with the warehouse makeover. They tell me how much I owe in labor costs since they're all putting their time in.

"Ty, man. Look, we bought this building together, and we need to finish it together. Your brother doesn't do any work, except whenever there's a backed-up toilet. We need you to put in some time."

So I move back to Atlanta to help finish off the warehouse. The plumbing is already run, so I begin to fix up this one spot, and while I'm doing it, I have to squat in the warehouse for a while before getting everything finished. The building has these big windows where I can create art while working on a kitchen and a bathroom. Soon I make this space look amazing, so sure enough, the guys suddenly want to charge me rent. FOR A BUILDING I OWN.

What?

"We would be renting it out to someone else if you weren't living there," they tell me.

"Yeah, but I physically put in the time and effort to fix it up. I paid for the materials and everything!"

"Yeah, well, we don't have any money coming in, so either pay us or get someone to fill the spot."

At this point, I've given up on the idea that fashion modeling is going to lead to any financial gain, or to even buying me a dinner. However, there are two other artistic ventures I've embarked on. Not only am I in a band, but I'm also making my first motion picture. And if you're wondering why you've never heard of either of these things, you'll soon learn why.

Whenever somebody asks what I consider myself, I have to stop to wonder, *Am I a carpenter? A designer? An artist? A photographer? An entertainer? A musician? A songwriter?* To this day, I'll say I have no idea what I am. But I do know what I'm drawn to. Music, of course, is one of those things.

During this period of time—1996–1997—I'm in a band with my brother called Butt Jowl Picnic. I know—epic name. (Remember this is all laying the foundation for where I'm at in life now.) The idea comes one day when I'm browsing through an old Farmer's Encyclopedia, which is, naturally, something I do all the time, and I see a diagram of the parts of the pig. Picnic, for example, is the part just below the shoulder that has a ton of fat in it, making it even more perfect in the band's title.

At first, I'm the frontman for Butt Jowl Picnic, writing most of the songs and basically doing everything. Wynn played the air conditioner since we didn't start out with a real drum kit. Eventually we brought in a real drummer, but let's face it, all drummers are crazy. He ended up stealing all our stuff, and in the book of Ty Pennington, which this just so happens to be, it sure seems par for the course. Wynn moved to keyboard where he'd hold down one note through the song. During the performances, I ran the projectors so we looked really cool, and sound guys would call us an "art band."

After playing and performing local gigs for a while—if they could be called that—Wynn comes to me with an idea.

"I've had a lot of feedback from the crowd," he says.

There isn't any "crowd"—it's more like a bunch of our friends in the bar. Nobody else wants to hear us, including our friends, but they simply suffer for our art.

"I'm hearing they want to see a little more of me," Wynn says.

"Oh, really?"

"Yeah. So why don't you sing all the sad, depressing love songs, and I'll do the fast, hard ones."

"That seems fair."

So sure enough, the first time Wynn performs, he puts on this '70s leisure suit with a rocking white belt and proceeds to become a Rodney Dangerfield on the stage, killing it. At one point while I'm jamming on the guitar, I look over and see him on the floor, gyrating and giving it his all.

"You're hired, man!" I tell him after the show.

Once Wynn begins singing my songs, he actually sees the brilliance behind him. At least he shows his appreciation late at night after having too much wine.

"Thank you, but you do know you're really drunk now, right?" I tell him.

Now that Wynn's taken over, he's realizing what my lyrics are all about.

"Is this about the night Dad threw ketchup at us?"

"Yeah, totally."

The lyrics are truly groundbreaking:

There's one thing I can't stand is up
Especially when I'm hit with ketchup

"That is *awesome*," he says.

"Yeah, it just came out."

Just like "Yesterday" by The Beatles, it only took a minute to write.

"You're really talented," Wynn says. (Actually, I think *the wine* says.)

We totally worship Devo, so we love bands that aren't just funny but also totally committed to their artistry. I remember Mark Mothersbaugh from Devo once saying that they're not a band but an actual movement of explanation of devolution. He says they're explaining why man is devolving.

I'm amazed by the commitment they make in going down that road with their music. When you pay to go see their shows, you don't just hear their songs; they change outfits six times, and they think out the rhythm, the dance moves, and the outfits that go with each particular song. I learn how an artist can think out methodically how the performance is going to go and how to incorporate different facets in different ways.

The other reason I'm drawn to bands like Devo and Ween is because of their sense of humor. They write songs with a sense of humor you don't find in other musicians. This is where I take my inspiration when it comes to music.

Even though Wynn never lets me take the lead again, I still have fun on the guitar in spite of being able to play only three chords. I can see how much joy it brings my brother, and looking back now, these are probably some of the best memories of my life. Honestly, I still miss those years. You're in a band and connecting with your brother. You're part of the art and the experiences together, living in the same spaces.

Then again, I don't miss them too much. 'Cause I'm squatting in a warehouse having to pay rent on a building I own, and my career is truly on a road to nowhere.

Inspiration, however, can be found in anything at any time.

"ONLY HAPPY WHEN IT RAINS"

"Hey, Ty, we need you to move all your [insert saucy adjective right here] piano parts again!"

As usual, Wynn is griping at me about my collection that I've been keeping for a few months. While squatting in the warehouse, I discover that every time it rains, the basement floods and the deserted pianos continue to fall apart. So these guys who own the pianos keep throwing huge pieces of the pianos away—chunks of ebony and structural parts that I see as potential furniture and candleholders. So I start saving all these parts they're wanting to get rid of, keeping them for future art projects. The only problem is that I put them in cardboard boxes that also get rained on, so then the boxes start to fall apart and become useless.

One day, while Wynn watches me trying to move a dozen of these boxes and they keep tearing open and dropping parts on the floor, he decides to be the loving brother he is and mock me.

"You know, Ty. You should probably give up on the boxes and switch to bags."

"You know, Wynn. That's a genius idea. What I should really do is box 'em, bag 'em, box 'em, bag 'em, box 'em, then just bag the whole thing."

"You should definitely bag the whole thing."

I stare at all these pieces of discarded pianos that I'm hoping to one day create art out of. But what if I never get the time to do it? I'm barely surviving as it is, so devoting time to making art out of pianos seems a bit far-fetched. I need to fix up the warehouse and clean things up instead of storing more junk.

Suddenly, in that moment, like Stanley Kubrick imagining *2001: A Space Odyssey* or Mel Brooks coming up with the idea behind *Spaceballs*, a flashbulb goes off in my head.

"You know, Wynn. You just gave me an idea about an artist who collects art but never creates art."

One of the reasons I decided to buy this warehouse in the first place is that I wanted to create a space where artists could make their art. In art school, I ended up meeting lots of people who were supposedly inspired by me. I guess they saw me constantly working on one project or another at my desk and thought it'd be cool to look busy and act like they have a purpose. Actually, I think they turn their lives into making art so they can feel the same elation I get when I have an idea and then watch it come to fruition.

So with that in the back of my mind, I start to imagine my grand movie idea inspired by Wynn and the piano parts.

His name is Adis Pozal. He is a brilliant German artist who takes the ideas he knows he'll never turn into art and wraps them in a bag. Then he puts them in a box, not having any idea what he will do with them, and then he puts them in another box. Finally, all these boxes go into one large black garbage bag. All these ideas are ones he'll never have the time to get to. But to Pozal, it's not the completion of the art that matters; it's the fact that the idea itself is there, and all you need to do is take it from there.

Adis Pozal decides to put on a show, so his installation is a big room in a warehouse, like the kind I'm living in. Scattered between the white walls and on top of the white floors lie all these large black garbage bags.

On the day before Pozal's big opening, the cleaning crew comes in and mistakes his artwork for garbage, hauling it away. When Pozal discovers that all his incredible ideas have been thrown away, he goes off the deep end, searching the city for the bags and shooting people with fart guns. When he finally gives up the futile search for his magnum opus, he wanders into a convenience store to buy a few items.

"Would you like a box or a bag?" the guy behind the counter asks him, causing Adis Pozal to become delirious.

Not only do I imagine this whole story, but I end up making this into a film, shooting it with my wonderful Handycam and actually editing it on a VCR tape, complete with shaky lines and terrible quality. No, you won't be able to find this particular film on IMDB.

For one particular scene where my brother plays an art dealer, I have a mock opening for a show and have all these actual artists come so I can interview them.

"So what do you think of Adis Pozal's influence over the art world?" I ask.

"Who? I thought these were just garbage bags in here."

While we're filming, an actual welder comes up to me with disbelief written all over his face.

"So let me get this straight," he says. "You put all this time and effort into this? Just to shoot a bird at the art world?"

Basically he's saying I've put all my time and effort into making this funny film instead of actually making art.

"Yes!"

"God bless you," he says.

This sums up my mind-set during those years. At this point in my life, the mid '90s, I'm collecting these pieces of pianos that most people consider trash. And I write *Adis Pozal*—a disposal. A film about how one man's trash is another man's treasure. I'm even wondering whether I should even do art, knowing there are other more important things, like landing a steady job and focusing on paying bills. Considering I've had to box and bag my fashion career, I come up with an artist who boxes and bags his ideas. So now I've made a movie about an artist who doesn't actually create art.

My modeling career is failing, and I'm failing in a band because we're not selling any tickets or getting paid, yet my other jobs are suffering because I'm in it. Even my neighbors' dogs who stay in the warehouse are showing me what they think of my music every day as they wander over by my amps and guitar chords. Chances are, when even the dogs are defecating on where you play music, you're failing.

I used everybody in my family in *Adis Pozal*. Now they're waiting for *Adis Pozal 2*. I can picture the opening scene with all these black garbage bags floating in the island of trash that's somewhere near Alaska and a boat approaching. Then you see Pozal finding his long-forgotten bags.

Makes me wonder, *What are those ideas I've forgotten about, those lofty ambitions and dreams that I never got to see?*

One day, maybe Adis Pozal can bring a few of those back to me.

"IS THIS IT"

People ask me all the time, "How'd you become Ty Pennington?" Here's the thing: I happen to believe in the famous quote, "If you want to get lucky, it pays to be prepared." I'm not sure who exactly said that, so why don't we just say it came from me, especially since I've been one lucky guy my entire career.

When I get that "lucky" call from my agent in 1999, I don't pick it up. The last time I spoke with them, I made it pretty clear about my feelings about auditions.

"Don't call me on any more stupid stuff that I know I'm not going to get," I tell them. "I have to put food on my table. I have to pay my rent. I have to stay in construction."

They know I'm building high-end furniture with a guy who went to Cooper Union, a private college in Manhattan specializing in architecture, art, and engineering degrees. I have things to do, and I don't want to be bothered with an audition.

My agent calls me back. "Look, Ty. I know you don't want to pick up the phone. But this time you really should audition for this. They're looking for a carpenter who really knows what he's doing and is kind of sarcastic."

Hmmm. Well, at least I'm half of that.

My audition goes well, but once again, I'm not the guy they're looking for.

"This is great," the producer tells me. "You're brilliant. But we're looking for your opposite type. You're skinny and attractive. We're looking for fat and funny."

Since when is it a bad thing to be skinny and attractive?

"Well, I was funny, right?"

"You're really funny, Ty, but we're looking for more of a fat guy," they tell me.

"Well, I can start eating immediately . . ."

They don't think it's going to work, and let's face it: I'll never be able to be the fat guy. Honestly, I don't know how actors can do it, gaining fifty pounds for a role. I can't ever seem to hold on to body fat. I'm sure once I turn sixty, it'll hit me right in the face.

So I go back to reality—to my building projects—but it doesn't take long before my agent calls again.

"Hey, man, thanks for the tip," I say before letting him talk. "Those guys clearly weren't looking for me. They needed a fat guy."

"No, Ty. That wasn't the audition we were talking about. You need to go down there to make a video of yourself that they can send off to a production company. Just a simple video of you building something on a construction project."

"Yeah, okay. Fine."

I look at the clock and wish there were more numbers to work inside of. All I can think about is finishing this massive job I'm right in the middle of, but I go ahead and give it another shot. My 324,892nd shot. Once I'm back in their office, they tell me they need to film me doing a remodel.

Oh, you want to get a tape of me that someone might not even watch or if they do, they'll probably yawn the entire time?

"All right. Let's go to the bathroom, and I'll act like I'm ripping out the toilet."

At this point, I'm pretty pissed about this whole thing. Another morning wasting my time. By the time I'm actually being filmed, I'm in full-bore Ty Pennington mode. Just to prove my point.

"Today we're going to rip out this toilet so we can put a TV in the crapper!"

I'm being over the top and overexpressive, wearing goggles and acting like I'm really going to toss this toilet out of the room. Really all I'm doing is being a big animated ball of high energy, screaming "let's do this!" to the viewer.

The camera crew let me be my spirited self, and they tell me that whatever the heck I just did works. They'll send it out. "Awesome. Thanks, guys. I gotta get back to my real job where I'm being paid like all of you."

Here's the thing: At this time in my life, nobody's asking me, "How'd you become Ty Pennington?" The only people who actually *know* about Ty Pennington are the ones working for the IRS. Every cent I'm earning seems to be going to them.

The truth is that I'm thirty-three years old and completely broke. I'm in debt to so many people, including the IRS. If I wasn't so honest back in the '80s, then maybe I wouldn't be habitually in financial dire straits. Some days I close my eyes and think of the naive and frankly stupid decision I made with the Internal Revenue Service.

When I lived in New York City and made those commercials, the money was spent as soon as I got it. One day, I walked into an H&R Block all sweaty and disoriented from a 105-degree fever. I almost collapsed as I wrote the IRS an IOU. I know—an IOU! Yes, you're right. This is the absolute worst possible move you could ever make. Good times. (I've been wondering what chapter this little story should go in. Oh yeah—Chapter 11!)

You know how sometimes you borrow a twenty from a friend, and then you forget about it and so do they? Well, the IRS is no such friend. They remember, even if months turn into years. They keep my homemade promissory note and keep adding on the late fees and the other penalties, until one day I learn exactly how much I owed. I get on the phone right away to talk with someone.

"Wait a minute—are you seriously kidding? Because I owed you $400 one day, I now owe you $28,000 today? I might as well never work again."

So I'm thirty-three and in quite a tough place. I really don't want to keep wasting time auditioning for cologne commercials that the pool boy next door is never going to get. My debt is so bad that I literally have to paint my shrink's house just to get medication in order to continue working.

Imagine a Russian accent, even though he's not Russian. "Ah, Ty . . . Whatever are we going to do with you, Ty? You're so talented."

I smile, give an "aw golly gee shucks" sort of shrug, and say, "Maybe we're going to let me paint your house?"

That's my dire straits. But then my agent calls. Again.

"About that audition. They called back, and now they want to see you in person."

All I can do is shake my head and utter a profanity of disbelief and annoyance.

"Cool. But I just told you I don't want to go on any more of these rabbit trails."

"Ty, this is a callback," he says. "This is good."

"Fine, but I'm in the middle of a kitchen. When do they want to see me?"

"Tomorrow."

My video had been sent to River Media in Knoxville, Tennessee. So that's where I need to drive to. My only problem is that I don't think my car is actually going to be able to make the three-and-a-half-hour drive. I did have an amazing 1960 Chevy, but someone must have thought it looked really cool and decided to steal it. My vehicle is a beater crammed full of all my tools and some lumber. So I borrow my girlfriend's Taurus wagon—with a good-luck duck on the dash—to take a trip that will literally change my life.

Here's the thing about auditions: there are countless people auditioning for something, and almost all of them will be rejected. Producers are looking for this one particular thing, and you never know what it might be. The frustrating thing is you don't know how to be better at what you do when you audition for a part; you can't do it better simply because you don't know exactly what they're looking for. You have to just be yourself.

And when you've been rejected so many times, and when they've chosen somebody else time after time, you eventually get to the point I was at. *Hey, guys, I really don't have time for this in my life.* It's really tough being in that profession. But then you get that one break that changes your life. So my advice to people: Keep going on auditions! You obviously can't not have another job at the same time, but don't give up.

The production company in Tennessee that wants to see me is casting for a new show that's a copy of a British show called *Changing Rooms*. I'm taking another chance because honestly, I have nothing else to lose. And that's a big emphasis on the word *nothing*.

When I walk into the auditioning room, I'm surrounded by a bunch of tall, good-looking men. Until now, I've been a little like Jim Carrey's character in *Dumb and Dumber*, thinking, *So you're telling me there's a chance!* But as I scan the room of hunks, I know this is just one more wasted trip. I'll be polite and do the audition and then get back to the job waiting for me in Atlanta.

I recognize a few of the guys from my time in Miami when I was working as an RV driver. As I walk around the room and see guys wearing brand-new tool belts that still have tags on them, I just smile and wait until I'm called.

This is really cool, but I have a kitchen to finish. Sure, this is all exciting, and I'm glad I drove up here, but really, I have legitimate things to do, people.

A friendly guy comes over and introduces himself. "Hey, I'm Frank."

"I'm Ty."

"Nice to meet you, Ty. Hey, why don't you build me a box?"

I scan the room and see from the wood they've stacked up that they clearly want me to build something simple, like a flower box. Without a second thought, I start to measure Frank's size, from his height and then his width and then seem to try to be judging his weight. While I'm doing this, the cameraman filming us can't help but laugh since he knows what I'm doing.

That's right . . . I'm about to build Frank a coffin. Immediately the two of us have chemistry.

That's a good life lesson to stop and share.

Here's the reality. Sometimes it's not about something happening when you least expect it. Sometimes something monumental happens when you absolutely and positively couldn't care less.

There were the days after art school when I was showing off whatever work I could, when I was overeager and telling people I'd do anything. "I'll work for free. Just give me a chance." But by this point, I was so tired of doing auditions and having the same response time and time again.

"Oh, you're just not quite right. We love you, but you're not that one. Go back and do whatever it was you were doing."

This is why I stopped doing auditions, why I'd given up on them. They used to be fun. Now they were just wasting my time.

This was the attitude I had when I ripped out that toilet, and it's the same one I have with Frank. Fortunately for me, it's very noticeable, and even better, this is exactly the sort of attitude they want in the carpenter they're looking for. They're looking for someone who's going to be overrun with too much to do and who gives quick, sarcastic answers to problems.

My newfound attitude is exactly what they're looking for.

So how'd I get a job being me? Well . . . I just acted like myself. I guess I was qualified.

Come to think of it, at this point in my life, I'm absolutely qualified. Let's do a quick overview:

1. I have experience in front of the camera. I know that a Levi's commercial isn't a television program, but I've still grown used to those lenses looking at me.
2. I know how to build stuff. This is something I'm already doing. In fact, if they don't hire me NOW, then I'm going to get back to building more stuff.
3. I have the sort of schedule that allows me to take time off at any given point since I'm freelancing. I've spent the last decade and a half freelancing.
4. I've also given up at this point in my career. I'm thirty-three years old, which is pretty late to start a career in television, but considering I've always looked twelve and that my maturity level is, let's face it . . . low, age isn't a deterrent.

So there's one more call I get. It's not someone asking me to advertise a bathing suit but someone who tells me the news.

"We want you to be our carpenter. What do you think?"

"I don't know what to think. But I'm excited to give it a shot."

Wow. Something worked. I'm not sure what, but they want me on their show.

Soon I receive an official email from one of the show's producers:

Dear Ty,

Congratulations. You have won the role of the handyman on TLC's new home improvement series *Trading Spaces*. I have no money in the budget for wardrobe, and you'll need to drive yourself to locations. Out of town, our hotels will be barely three-star, and there's no on-set catering. We'll be working long hours with no overtime, and you won't get top billing. But we're really glad to have you on the show and looking forward to getting started.

Sincerely,

Leigh Seaman, Executive Producer

PS: Can you bring your own toolbelt until we find a tool sponsor?

No money in the budget? Need to drive myself to locations? Three-star hotels and no catering? Sure doesn't sound like some monumental TV show that's going to change my life and launch my face into the stratosphere and into pop culture. I don't even know if they're going to show it outside the state of Tennessee. There's no way I can ever imagine this show is going to produce a genre that's going to grow to be a massive success.

All I know is that if you want to get lucky, it pays to be prepared.

Day

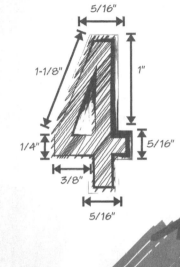

WALLS AND LINES

Walls and Lines

"DIRTY DEEDS DONE CHEAP"

'm pretty sure one of the first words my parents ever taught me was the word *job*. They used it often and tended to repeat it over and over in sentences.

"We all have JOBS to do, and your JOB is to keep your room clean," Mom tells me. "Another JOB you can do is wash the dishes," my stepfather chimes in. They'll even go as far as to say, "Congratulations, you've been promoted and have a new JOB title—maintenance engineer, aka janitor, aka bathroom cleaner." Which, of course, as a five-year-old, I consider to be a big deal. I eagerly clean around the toilet (inside and out). Next the sink, and then I do the finishing touch of hanging the washrag back on the towel rack next to the sink. This particular placement eventually is followed by a loud exclamation and the inevitable loss of that particular JOB the moment my mother uses that rag to wash her face before bed. She actually never recovers from that moment and now always brings a clean, fresh towel with her every time. Some surprises you really learn from after you've been fired.

Come to think of it, I will lose almost every JOB I ever have, and I will end up having quite a few. I think it's interesting that I end up with, let's face it, an amazing DREAM JOB where I make dreams come true by using my hands and sometimes my heart.

What's also interesting is that I start out dreaming of a job where I basically just use my feet. That's right, at about the age of six or seven, I start playing football or, as they call it in the US, soccer. Yes, I dream of walking into a sold-out arena with fans chanting my name. People singing victory songs as Ty Pennington pulls off miracle athletic feats, bicycles, scissor kicks, and diving headers, scoring countless goals and receiving praise along with shiny golden awards that I raise above my head as I say I couldn't have done it without the support of all of you. Well, let's just say that not all dreams come true. Or maybe they do, but they just sometimes take a different route on the way toward the goal.

In reality, it will be my hands instead of my feet that will work countless hours, not only to help build those dreams, but also to build the shelves to set those awards on.

My first job after being a bathroom cleaner will break all child labor laws, but wow . . . I'll love it and consider it the best thing in my life. It's being a print-maker. Basically I'm printing art. What? Yes, that's right. Age ten. Printmaker. Artist. Life is amazing. I work at a local press located in an old building on the outskirts of Atlanta. It's run by a peculiar old guy that I help to print silk screens, old-school letterpress, gigantic posters of music festivals, and all the way to propaganda posters. The work environment consists of loud music drowning out the sounds of the rhythmic printing press, matched in equal volume by the eye-watering fumes of the printer's ink.

Once again, I'm ten years old, so of course this is an awesome first job. Well, except for lunch that's always Brunswick stew from the BBQ joint across the street. Lovely but basically slop. Honestly, I had it every day. Let's face it, sometimes you may lose your lunch and lose your job. We all need change. And after a change of address, aka my parents uprooting us to the distant suburbs, my lunch and my job are both lost. Come to think of it, so am I. At least for a short while.

My second job, and my first in suburbia, is as a lawn mower—a thankless job where the average pay is five dollars a yard. Seriously, let's talk about child labor laws. I mean, yes, it's barely 1978, but five dollars to mow one lawn? Who came up with that number? If that's not terrible enough, this particular job causes my parents to fear that I'll lose my foot simply by mowing over it and sending blood and flesh shooting out with the blades of grass. This type of positive thinking on the part of my parents is another reason kids with ADHD have such confidence in themselves and seem to be accident-prone.

Oh boy. Now there are two words that sum up my life—"accident-prone."

Yes, I've always been prone to mistakes, but it's no accident that I'm only paid five dollars to mow an acre of grass in the southern August heat while almost dying of a heat stroke. And speaking of gaffes, I think I may have just made a blunder by mixing some metaphors while intending to throw in a pun. What a lapse of miscalculation!

Speaking of strokes, that job was thankless but not crankless, since it introduces me to the art of using crank-start tools. This will naturally prepare me for my next real job. (And no, working at Wendy's for two weeks doesn't really count, considering all I did was throw free food to anyone coming by the drive-thru until I was quickly let go.) My next job is the rough and manly job of being a professional landscaper, a job where I first hear the roar and rev of crank-start power tools. Yes! Feeling first-hand the thundering torque of edgers, hedgers, mowers, and blowers, or in other words, experiencing the raw power of digging in the dirt. All for the amazing rate of three dollars an hour. Yeah. Okay, fine . . . $3.50 an hour. Good times.

Some jobs in my life don't last very long. Like working at an Italian restaurant for a day. Anytime I go into a restaurant to try to become a waiter, they tell me the same thing: "You look like a busboy."

"I promise you, I'm a waiter," I always tell them.

In the case of this Italian restaurant, they're hard to convince.

"You really look like a busboy."

"I know I look like I'm twelve, but I'm actually twenty!"

"Yeah, but we need a busboy."

When I finally get my first table, I bring out a tray loaded with glass mugs full of beer. As this bald guy is looking at me with fear and trepidation on his face, all the mugs tip over, one by one, right onto his head. As I see his face turn red, I walk back to the kitchen and drop off my apron.

Another waiter job I get is right after landing a modeling gig in New York. I decide I need some regular income, so I start working at a Mexican restaurant. On the day I start, their dumbwaiter breaks, so here I am, carrying all these dirty, heavy ceramic plates up and down three floors' worth of stairs. The work is so grueling on that first night that I tell them at the end of the shift that I don't think this job is for me.

"You know what? Don't even put me on the taxes. This is a freebie. This is on me. I gave you tonight for free."

Sometimes you have to work in a position in order to realize it's just not your calling in life, even if you're only in it for five or six hours. Not long after this, I begin to start landing more and more modeling jobs. So each job I've ever lost or left has led to another one.

As I always say, choose a job you love, and you'll never have to work a day in your life. Okay, fine . . . that's a quote from Confucius. But it's one I live by.

Here's another one from Milton Berle that sort of defines my life: "If opportunity doesn't knock, build a door."

As I always say, choose a job you love, and you'll never have to work a day in your life. Okay, fine . . . that's a quote from Confucius. But it's one I live by.

"STUCK IN THE MIDDLE WITH YOU"

So I'm flying to Chicago to film an episode of *Trading Spaces*. Man, I seem to really like taking on projects in the middle of other projects. You know what they say: "If you want something done, give it to the busiest person."

Which brings me back to another project I'm doing while in the middle of all these other projects. Yeah. It's called writing a book in seven days. Ha. No joke.

I'm on Day Four.

How am I doing? You still there?

Think we'll make the deadline?

"CLIMBING UP THE WALLS"

On Day Three of *Extreme*, the framing is started and the walls are put up, so on Day Four, you begin to see the house fully framed.

The first framing job I ever complete is the three-story tree house we build in our backyard when I'm nine years old. It all starts with a loose leg—a piano leg. Funny how piano parts have become instrumental in my life at certain moments. One day I notice this wobbly leg, so I yank it off and use it to build something up. I prop up the piano with a stick and some bricks. My parents aren't happy.

"Okay, Mr. Creative," Mom says. "From now on, if there's any sort of project you're going to do, take it outside."

Mom's favorite phrase to Wynn and me is "take it outside." As I've already shared, I've been into demolition my whole life, so my parents finally have enough and tell me, "No more wrecking the house." This gives me an idea: I'm going to build a massive tree house. I have a vision of it in my mind and know what it needs to look like. I want to prove I can build something.

If you don't understand what I'm doing inside, wait till you see what I do outside.

There's one problem. Since my dad is a jazz musician, he has no tools in his house. Absolutely none. My brother and I might be able to find stuff to fix bikes, but that's about it. Some kids I know have mechanics for fathers who enjoy helping their boys build things.

Like a Boy Scout I know who has his father build their pinewood derby car. I'm proud that I built my own pathetic version of a car with my own hands, and I'm proud that I stand up to the kid and accuse his father of building his car. A bunch of the other boys are cheating. Am I proud enough to bite the kid's ear off and get kicked out of Boy Scouts? No. But at least I'm standing up for my rights, right?

A friend of ours has a mechanic for a father, and his go-kart ends up having axle bearings and grease and flies, while ours sputter along way behind. I'm amazed and remember thinking, *Wow, so that's what engineering and tools can do for your go-kart!*

For the tree house, I decide we have to have the right tools, so I decide to barter with people to get their help. Wynn and I collect comics, learning from some older guys who teach us how to do it so we know what they can be worth. Basically I end up bartering comics for time with my friends' dad's tools. Then Wynn and I start in the morning and finish at the end of the day. The three-story tree house contains a sunroof, a balcony, and the whole nine yards. When my mother finally walks out and looks at it in amazement, I tell her to keep walking.

"I'm sorry, ma'am. The press interviews are over."

I'm so delighted with the tree house that I spend the night out there and proceed to get eaten alive by the swarming mosquitoes. Wynn can't take it, so he leaves early. All I can think of is how proud I am to be sleeping—or trying to sleep—in a structure I actually built. Not only that, but I brought a community together and convinced them to grab their tools, and in just one day, we built a tree house that the entire neighborhood can enjoy and share. Talk about some foreshadowing for later in life. But these are the little bitty moments in life that shape and form who you become.

Speaking of shapes and forms . . .

Once you've framed the house and you run the electrical and plumbing lines throughout, it's time to put up the walls. Honestly, walls have always been a part of my life. I drive my mom and father and pretty much everybody in my family up the wall. Which makes complete sense to then spend most of my life running rollers, brushes, and everything else up walls. Including ideas. Not only do I send my parents up walls, but I also end up sitting or leaning against the wall in the school hall pretty much most of the year. A lot of people tell me, "Don't you see the writing on the wall, Ty?" Truth is, the writing on the wall is my own writing. To this day, most of the time it's illegible.

It always takes that special someone to see between the lines, to discover the potential, to somehow picture more in the writing. Mom knows I'm creative because I love drawing on the walls. It's interesting that I end up finding a career later in life where the main thing I do is add art to walls. I've been doing that my entire life!

Let's face it. With ideas, you throw them against the wall and hope some of them stick. Boy, did I throw a lot of waste against the wall.

Sometimes those crazy ideas get you somewhere. Like how destroying a toilet lands me on this new show called *Trading Spaces*.

"BLISTER IN THE SUN"

"They're filming the pilot in Lawrenceville, Tennessee," one of the producers for *Trading Spaces* tells me. "You may want to drive up and check out the set. You know—get to know the crew a little and get an idea of what you're walking into."

It's a great idea, so I do exactly that. When I arrive at the house in Lawrenceville where they're filming an episode that's actually ahead of the initial pilot for *Trading Spaces*, a show I doubt ever airs, everybody is already running around busy and has no clue who I am. Or maybe they just were too busy to care. I walk up to someone just to let them know I'm there.

"Hey, I'm Ty Pennington and I'm going to be a carpenter on the next episode. I wanted to come and meet a few people."

"Great!" I'm told as they rush away with work to do.

I wouldn't say I have the look of a carpenter. At this point in my life, I'm still in my band phase. Remember, I'd given up on my modeling career, so being on a television show was the furthest thing from my mind and my hair's mind. I'd grown my hair long on the side but short on the top and front. (My look was definitely mod, as in 1960s pre-punk.) I was growing up. I remember meeting a young woman at a club once who couldn't stop looking at my do.

"What is up with your hair?"

"I don't know," I tell her. "I'd say it's more down than up."

"Oh, it's definitely down," she says.

"Kinda jealous, are you?"

"No. Not at all."

It's got a cool, '60s rock-and-roll look to it. Think of guys from Oasis. So when I show up to see everybody, not only am I donning this artsy, androgynous haircut, but I'm wearing a sleeveless T-shirt and shorts three sizes too big that hang down to my knees and are held up by a cinched belt. I'm a combination of the '90s "rap meets grunge," aka "Li'l Oxy Moron."

For a few moments I stroll around the lawn, trying to be a casual observer. I'm looking for the producers, or really anybody I can connect with. At one point I see a Latino woman under a tree, sitting on a chair and working quietly on a sewing machine.

"Excuse me?" I ask. "Do you speak English?"

Dark eyes quickly shoot up at me as she says yes.

"Cool. I'm one of the carpenters for the show, and I'd like to meet some people. Can you tell me where the producers or designers are?"

"Yes, I could," she says while focusing on the piece of fabric she's sewing. For a moment I wonder if she's actually going to tell me. "They're in the house."

"Thank you. Gracias."

"De nada."

The moment I enter the house, I hear this tough brunette yelling at someone moments before I'm introduced to her. Amy Wynn Pastor is the carpenter on this episode, and as I said, this is the debut episode *before* the debut, one that I don't think ever airs because every single thing seems to be going horribly wrong. All I keep hearing are people shouting, "This isn't how it's done!" and looking either frustrated or confused or both. The homeowners appear to be in their seventies, much older than I initially expect. All I can think is, *What's going on here?* The entire crew talks in this really thick Tennessee accent.

"Hay. Y'all need to gat in dare and undo dat carpat."

I just watch like a kid in a movie theater eating popcorn with my eyes wide open, thinking, *Wow!*

Nobody talks to me because they're all so busy with everything, and I'm told the executive producer is at the other house and is going to be here at lunch. They tell me to hang out in the yard and I'll be able to see the producer at lunch. Since it's an hour-and-a-half drive back home to Atlanta, I decide to stick around. I find a lawn chair, take off my shirt, and start sunning on the driveway. This, of course, will always be how the rest of the crew describes my first day of work on *Trading Spaces*. Imagine what they're thinking.

"Hey, did you meet the new carpenter?"

"Yes, what a . . ."

I show up and don't do any work, and I'm just there oiling up under the sun. But the truth is, there's nothing for me to do. I don't know anybody here, and I've never been introduced to any of them. Nobody's asking me to help simply because they have no idea why I'm here.

When the producer shows up, she approaches me with the Hispanic woman I'd met earlier.

"Hey, Ty. I want you to meet somebody. This is Hildi, our designer."

"Oh, we've already met," Hildi says as she gives me a delightful smile. *Oh, what the . . .*

The woman I see at the sewing table who I assume must be the South American help and who I spoke to like she's a hired hand who might not even speak English is Hildi Santo-Tomas, one of the talented designers on the show. Considering how busy she is and how I look, it's no wonder she didn't stop what she was doing to chat with the new carpenter. She was probably thinking, *What a cute boy they sent us—he must be a PA to help load the truck.*

When I get back home to Atlanta, my girlfriend asks how the trip went.

"Good. But honestly, I think I'm on a show called 'Redneck Remodeling' because everybody has a real Southern accent."

"Oh," she says with doubt in her voice.

"Or maybe it'll be great," I tell her.

Honestly, though, at this point I have no idea what the outcome is going to be and how the show will do.

On my official first day on *Trading Spaces* (and not when I'm sunbathing while watching Hildi sweat at the sewing machine), I'm working with a designer who basically introduces himself by saying, "I just need you to know . . ."—and then proceeds to list off one thing after another that I need to build for him.

"And I need it as soon as possible," he says.

"That's great. What's your name again?" I ask.

"My name's Doug."

"Great. My name's Ty. I just need to clear something up. I work *with* you, not *for* you. I don't know if you know this, but my contract says *talent*."

He nods and dismisses my comment. "Yeah, yeah, whatever. I understand. I'm just saying these are all the things I need."

"Sounds like we're going to be talking about your needs a lot in this episode," I tell him, not trying to be funny but just being my regular self. In a tone that says, *Looks like you're going to have lots of needs on this show, Doug, but I'm going to have a few myself.*

Doug Wilson looks at me and seems to be thinking, *Oh, so this is how things are going to go.* I'm a little worried that our chemistry isn't going to work out so well. But this is how things go with Doug and me; I'm going to call him out for being a jerk (PG term) because, let's face it, that's what he's really good at being. Soon enough, I realize this is perfect. Doug is our antagonist, the villain on the show. Every hero needs a nemesis.

The cool thing about *Trading Spaces* is the variety pack of personalities and styles that each one brings. So as I said, Doug is sort of our villain. Lori brings her Southern belle charm. Hildi is absolutely nuts. Genevieve Gorder is a very creative graphic designer. And then there's Frank, who one day tells me, "I'm not a designer; I'm a florist." The variety is amazing to me.

When I get that first call, I don't realize that the producer, Leigh Seaman, had taken the tapes of all the potential carpenters and shown them to her husband, Matt.

"I think there's something about that guy," Matt tells her while watching my audition tape. "Women will probably want to see him build their things, and guys will just want to sit down with him and have a beer."

The good thing is, Leigh agrees with her husband. Honestly, things could've gone so many different ways. When we're all auditioning, all we know is that you're a carpenter who's helping other designers build a room. I've given up on this industry and my modeling career. I'm not even sure if I'm handsome. I'm cute, and there's a big difference. I look like a puppy. I'd be hired to be the son of a guy half my age. So my attitude is, "Yeah, Frank. Sure. I can build you a box. Maybe six feet tall, one that you eventually put in the ground . . ." I just wanted to get it over with, because I really did have work waiting for me back home. Maybe I don't seem as eager as one should be at an audition, but I think in life this is exactly what happens. The busiest person (or person who *seems* the busiest) is the one they end up choosing. Maybe this makes me look confident, something everybody likes.

Then again, my sarcastic attitude seems to be the thing they want.

Oh, a box. How original. How unique.

That's exactly the sort of attitude they need for the role.

So being deep in debt and busy trying to pay it off while also giving up on my modeling career force me to go back to what I've always done and what I've always been good at—working with my hands. When the audition comes along, I don't have to convince them I'm a carpenter. This is my job and what I'm doing for a living.

Basically, I get a job being *me*. Being the guy who builds and designs things and can also be sarcastic with others. Who knew they were looking for someone just like that? Ultimately, I'm actually experienced in all three categories:

1. Knowing how to build things.
2. Being comfortable in front of the camera.
3. Making people feel comfortable in front of the camera, which I find out later is even more important when I'm dealing with homeowners and people who've never been on TV. The ability to make people comfortable on camera changes the whole thing, and to this day, I still think it's my greatest gift.

"PEOPLE ARE STRANGE"

It's funny. When I first hear the title for *Trading Spaces*, of course I think of one of the funniest movies ever made—*Trading Places*. It's a hilarious story about a homeless man with nothing who meets a wealthy man with everything, and their lives get completely switched in the process. Which is, interestingly enough, exactly what happens to my life since I'm literally almost homeless before I get on *Trading Spaces*. I'm in such debt and owe so many people money.

It's funny if you ask anybody who knew me back then to comment on what happens to me in the next five or ten years. They will all be like, "That lucky plucker! How the pluck did that happen? He was squatting in a warehouse the last time I saw him, peeing into Gatorade bottles and moving his duffle bag from one place to another!" Nobody, including me, can ever imagine I'd get a break quite like this.

So the title *Trading Spaces* is ironic, since I literally end up trading the space I'm living in for another. But it's still not an easy journey once I get on the show.

Trading Spaces is truly groundbreaking because for the first time ever in a do-it-yourself show, we put tools in the hands of homeowners and make them believe they can do it. In doing so, we're making the world believe, "Hey, if they can do it, so can I!" This is truly what a DIY show stands for—to create that belief inside that, yes, you *can* and *will* do this.

There are a few other shows on television, like *This Old House*, that present the house beforehand and then reveal what it looks like after, but you rarely get to see the process. The format of *TS* is new to America, where homeowners are not only doing the work, but they're also forced to work with a designer they didn't choose. Add to that the fact that you're switching houses with neighbors and spending the night in their house, and you suddenly have riveting television.

Here are some behind-the-scenes facts you may not know about *TS*. The idea comes from a popular show in the UK called *Changing Rooms*. Now British shows are always pretty unique, simply because of their personalities and sense of humor. In the UK, you have houses that are like a hundred thousand years old. So the idea of changing rooms in them takes on a whole new meaning. Plus, even though the homeowners' reactions are always negative, the Brits almost never show any emotion. And their definition of getting angry will be something like, "Oh no, I don't believe we can have tea this weekend a'tall."

The company behind *Changing Rooms* isn't using that format in America, so the Discovery Channel purchases the format and gets the rights to produce their own version. Of course, nobody expects the show to be as popular as it becomes. The mind-blowing thing is that it becomes incredibly popular, even though it's coming on at four o'clock in the afternoon. With the rise of cable and all these new channels, people suddenly have all these options. Of course, I've never even heard of the network the show is on until I get on the show. Yes, we all know Discovery, but back then, *TS* is on The Learning Channel—not TLC, as it's eventually called.

To me, *Trading Spaces* really is the show that makes people cry for the wrong reasons. *Extreme* will make them cry for all the right reasons, but on *TS*, it will be more like, "What have you done to my room?" So naturally, we cannot ever talk about *TS* without mentioning some of those memorable surprises (aka FAILS)—those awe-inspiring moments when we get to basically say, "Surprise! We've stapled hay to your walls!" The truth is that bad ideas can sometimes look good, but the pros watching at home are still probably shaking their heads and saying it's terrible.

There are so many memorable scenes. Like the woman who hates that we paint her fireplace and acts as if her world is ruined. The best part is her husband just shaking his head, saying, "Uh-uh, she ain't right." I know how simple this is to fix. You just pull that sleeve off it and start over. I'm in the background just watching, laughing at reactions like this. You work so hard on each room, so you're not leaving before you see the reaction.

And there's the people who end up fighting and wrestling just because of the room color. "You painted it brown! You know I hate brown!" I still laugh about it now. Or the time we end up designing a kitchen with a thousand wine labels, only to discover the family doesn't drink alcohol. I spend many hours helping the family peel off our wonderful art. In fact, a lot of my memories of *Trading Spaces* consist of helping families clean up after the work we've done.

Here's the thing with crying: you can't tell if someone's happy or sad. When you finally see their reaction, all you're wondering is whether they love it or hate it. Sometimes they're crying for the wrong reason, and sometimes I'm laughing for the wrong reason too (since I'm in the back watching). It's not my fault; I'm just the lowly carpenter.

The thing with *Trading Spaces* is you have to do something that's never been done, but in doing so, sometimes the homeowners don't appreciate your creativity. Sometimes the anger boils over. For instance, in the show's first season, a designer named Dez Ryan ends up remaking a room with a lot of metal—like metal lampshades and stainless-steel trash cans. The homeowner is so furious when he sees her that we have to get her off the set and out of there. No joke. He's telling people he wants her killed off by the mob. "I know people." It's almost as if she won't make it through the night if we don't intervene and get her out of there.

There's also the well-known wrestling match one neighbor has with another about her choice of color. Sure, the homeowner warns their neighbor about using the color brown, but still. This shows that color can definitely affect your mood.

The epic fails happen more times than I can count. You're building a beautiful bed, and it's looking amazing; then you try to bring it into the house and realize it's not going to fit in the door. So you have to cut it in half and splice it back together, which is such a great idea, especially since there will be a seam right on the headboard. Sure, it may be covered up eventually, but you'll know it's there. Or you may be using the wrong kind of materials, like painting latex over oil (meaning it's not going to stick!).

I will venture to say anytime you bring sand into someone's home and act like it's a beach theme, they'll look at you with dumbfounded faces that say, *You really dumped eighteen hundred bags of sand in this room? And you think with four kids this is a good idea?* Yeah, that's going to be an epic fail. But don't tell that to Hildi, who doubles down on her straw room.

Here are some of the comments about these memorable fail moments on *Trading Spaces*:

* "We have to put helmets on our kids."
* "The thing above the bed has got to go."
* "I gotta get used to it."
* "It's straw . . ."
* "Aaaragahrhrha!"
* "I'm going to have to leave the room."
* "I don't even know where to start."
* The sounds of desperate wailing in the room next to us.

Sometimes we have to draw a line at the hostility toward our rooms, resulting in scenes never making it on television. For instance, there's one time we give a kid everything he ever asks for, and then when he sees it, he throws a temper tantrum. "I hate it!" he screams, while all of us know this isn't making it on the show. Don't kids change their minds every hour? That's the funny part about even daring to ask what they want their room to look like.

The anger and frustration aren't always reserved for the homeowners. I remember a hilarious moment when one of the personalities on the show got irked by me on maybe the second or third show. I was probably saying and doing something sarcastic (imagine that!), and after the scene, they come up to my face with fury in their eyes.

"You just stole that scene!"

"Well, I can give it back."

I didn't realize this was something you could do—actually stealing a scene.

"A HARD DAY'S NIGHT"

Every song's been sung, every story told, every movie made, every piece of art painted. Well, okay . . . not really. But in the world of making furniture and remodeling rooms and homes, let's face it, pretty much everything *has* been done before. So whatever you do, you want to make sure it's done differently so you feel you've come up with something original. That's what I love about *Trading Spaces*.

You're forced to work with nothing. You're forced to work with less. To make something out of nothing.

The title of this book should really be *Making Something out of Nothing*. Those are the skills I'm forced to learn for shows like *Trading Spaces*. Up to that point in my life, I've had a shop where we make high-end furniture with a guy who went to Cooper Union. You're talking about the kind of joinery that involves working with table saws with blades down to thirty-two inches and glue and no screws whatsoever and high-end mortise and tenon joints.

Then I'm suddenly going to work with an old table saw on an unlevel yard or a driveway with extension cords running through water. I'm using one of only two finish nailers we have for the show, the kind that are made with CO_2 cartridges, so when one of them jams, the entire show is shut down.

But not only are the tools I'm using cheap, I'm forced to have to come up with ideas quickly and execute them even more quickly. Oh, and I'm supposed to be building beautiful pieces of furniture with all the money the designers have left, which is usually between $40 and $60.

Oh, you want three pieces of furniture? Great! I can't wait to see what that looks like.

Makes me think of when The Beatles were forced to play every night in Hamburg in their early years, sometimes playing for four or five hours until late into the night. They were unknowns playing cover songs, and they learned to do all different types of music simply because they were tired of playing the same old songs night after night. During the process, they began writing their own tunes as well. Some of those nights on *Trading Spaces* (and later on *Extreme*) certainly were "A Hard Day's Night" as we'd be working late hours. Yes, you're working your butt off and it's wearing you out, but finally the room turns out looking amazing.

Not long after getting on *Trading Spaces*, I'd realize something—for the first time, my spirits are actually being lifted by being at work. I really have so much fun at my job. I'm in my element, doing what I'm

born to do. Every single job, I get to create something new and different. I'm working with designers, yet I'm able to build pieces to show to the world—the viewers on television. Sure, I can't help but be frustrated at times because I'm the carpenter and not a designer, and yet more and more designers would come and throw me a bone.

"Here's $300, Ty. Why don't you design something cool you want to show off?"

"I love you so much!" I tell them.

Nobody does that for anybody, not in this industry, and yet . . . when it does happen, which becomes more and more, I know this is a moment I have to shine. I live for these opportunities where I'm allowed to have creative freedom to come up with something really awesome. So every time, I go above and beyond to create something amazing. And because I love doing this, the final piece usually sticks out. Kinda like after all those early shows The Beatles do, they start writing and performing their own stuff—incredible songs like "I Saw Her Standing There."

I've said it before, but if there's ever a job designed so perfectly for someone, it's the job I get on *Trading Spaces*. I'm working outside in barely any clothes, forced to work with barely anything I'm accustomed to tool-wise and budget-wise and time-wise, and I'm doing it all in three days and then moving on to another project. Not only leaving the house we're at but leaving a particular town to go to another. For a guy with ADHD, I don't have time to get bored and understimulated. Everything about this job is change and busyness and creative explosions of the brain.

Yes, the perfect job, one that doesn't really even exist before mine on *Trading Spaces*. We end up spawning so many shows that TV carpenters become a commodity that Hollywood is looking for. I can't believe it.

I've become a commodity. I wish I could clone myself.

The truth is *Trading Spaces* really shows me the sort of person I've always believed I can be. I just didn't know exactly what he looked like.

Back when I'm in art school, I have a vision for who I want to be—a graphic designer who wins awards, one known for being one of the very best at his craft. Along the way, however, I learn I don't want to sit behind a desk for the rest of my life. I love being outside working under clear skies, and I don't know if I can ever give that up. The only way I get to this point is by improvising like a jazz musician.

I think I've pretty much been improvising my way through life.

I have a friend who's had a career of doing that too. If you're a handyman these days, someone calls you to build a deck, and then while you're working on it, they say, "Hey, can you also do marble floors?" You're not going to say no, right? You say "Yeah, of course I can!" Then you go out and study everything you can about marble floors since it's the first time you're doing it. Naturally, you're going to improvise. You just don't let anybody know about it.

That's the way I've been my whole life. "Sure, I can do that!" even though I have no idea what I'm doing.

Let's get a little deeper for a moment.

I look at life like this. And maybe it's because I lived in Japan or maybe because I love the psychedelic jazz band Syd Arthur. I think life is like a stream or a trickle of water. Because people will say, "I got off my path" or "I'm on the wrong path" or "I'm heading down the right path." So if your life is a stream of water heading down a path, it hits a rock and can split off in two different directions. Whether it's a choice in a relationship or a job.

And yeah, by the way, I do get into my romantic, personal relationship stuff on a later day. I mean a future chapter. You know what I mean.

Perhaps you're heading down a path with someone else, or let's say your stream is heading in the same direction as another's. Sometimes these two streams can go in separate directions, but who's to say they're not going to meet up again and continue a journey that's now gained extra current because it's gone off in two directions?

My theory in life: Don't be afraid of the boulder in your way. Know that it's eventually going to be there. Realize it's sending you in another direction. Maybe you're avoiding something behind it that's even worse. Maybe you're going around something instead of hitting a wall.

"FAME"

We don't have Facebook, Twitter, and Instagram to show us the popularity of *Trading Spaces* after it first comes out. The only way I begin to hear about its popularity is from others who are reading about it and

My theory in life: Don't be afraid of the boulder in your way. Know that it's eventually going to be there. Realize it's sending you in another direction.

talking to others in chat rooms online. What really confirms the show's popularity is when I'm shopping in Orlando at thrift stores, and twenty-something, tattooed hipsters cruising on low-rider bikes shout out greetings to me.

"Hey, man, you're Ty," one of the dudes says.

"Hey, yeah. How's it going?"

"Dude, we love your show, bro," the other guy says.

At first I don't even believe this. "You guys watch that show?"

"Yeah, man. Every day at four."

This is when I know the show has really caught on, after realizing that hip and artsy young people like these guys are watching a daytime do-it-yourself show on television. By the end of the second season, our popularity is obvious when more and more people begin to show up on our set after we arrive in a new town. People start bringing their family and coolers and snacks and lawn chairs. I begin to feel like an animal in a zoo . . . who's hoping to be fed peanuts.

"Oh, hey, everybody! Ty's using the band saw!" Or "Look, he's got the power sander out! This is going to be exciting!"

In the third season, on a Friday or Saturday night, the crowd is larger and louder than usual, and things are starting to get weird. They apparently have been drinking for a while and are starting to get a bit rambunctious and restless, with people yelling for me to take off my shirt and more flashbulbs lighting up the darkness. When we start to do the reveal, there's only one way to go in and out of the house we're working on, and the crowd is making it impossible for any of us to go back to our trucks on the street. Once we finish up, I'm flanked by crew members through the crowd with a garbage can over my head. I'm suddenly going back to my roots when I was dumpster diving.

The moment is surreal. Looking back, this has got to be one of the most exciting moments for me on the show. This is what rock stars feel like, with all these people wanting to get to me. But I'm also wondering, *Whose idea was it to use this trash can? I've got garbage juice dripping all over my body. Wouldn't it be better if I just waved good-bye?*

So as I climb in my truck soiled in dumpster juice with everybody waving and some people flipping me off since I didn't stop, I tell the crew members, "Guys, I can stop and take some pictures."

"There's no way!" they tell me. "There's too many of them."

There's a lot, but still. I'm confused why they're rushing me out. I think everybody's just getting caught up in the craze of popularity of the show. As I leave the throng of people, I realize what's happened.

Wow, I may just have become a household name.

One who currently smells like banana peels, sour beer, and barbeque chicken.

Not long after this, I'm going out on my first book tour, and the line in the bookstore ends up being so big that the fire marshal is called and he shuts down the event. It's crazy and ironic too. Early in my life, all I crave is attention, but then you get it, and you think, *Oh, I don't want it* that *much.* Sure, deep down you want to be loved and well-known, or at least to be well-liked. But there is such a thing as being satisfied.

I suddenly am the guy who, every time I go into a home improvement store—which basically is like every single day of my life—gets greeted by people who say, "Hey, Ty!" (Which makes it sound like they've known me for ten years.) Not only do they know me, but they also know what I do, so I'm the guy that people are asking questions to in aisles 7, 8, and 9.

"Ty, by the way, would you use a three-fourths-inch converter down to a half inch?"

"Yeah, I think I would."

Day

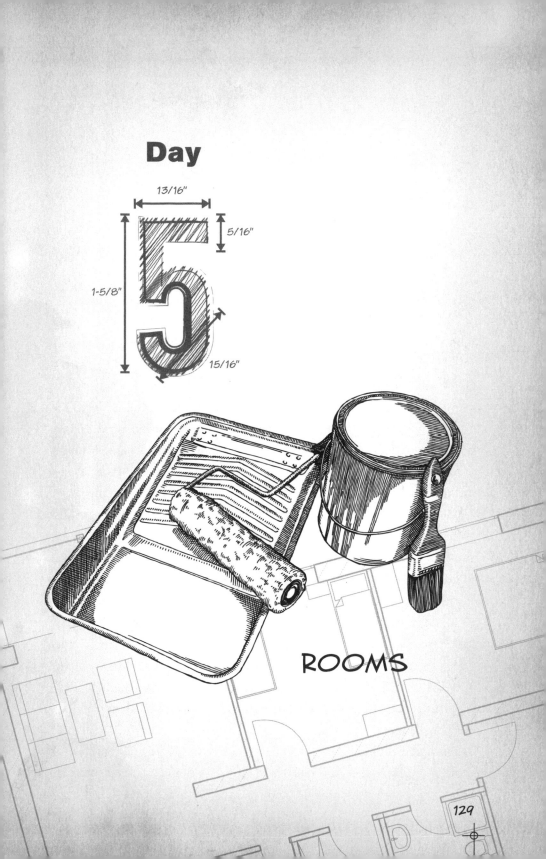

ROOMS

Rooms

"FOURTH OF JULY"

The sound of framing a house is oddly comforting to me. It's the sound of woodwork and progress, a place I would return to over and over in my life . . . always ready and able to swing a hammer. It's also loud, which is an environment I enjoy. Because after all, loud turns into chaos, and chaos turns into fun. I may have been able to build a three-story tree house as a kid, but seeing what an amazing bunch of hardworking humans with nail guns can do in a day . . . Honestly, I've seen miracles happen in one day. Like an entire framed home having its roof laid. It's hard work; it's hot; and it's a whole lot of hammering, yet at the end of the day you may even have a framed room to relax in after all that hammering.

Wow. I just realized how long I've been framing—hammering nails, turning screws, and banging boards together. Honestly, I love building things big and small, and framing. Come to think of it, I've been framed for almost everything that's gone wrong in my childhood. I mean everything. Broken window—Ty did it. Broken faucet—Ty did it. You get the idea. Maybe that's why I end up so handy. I have to fix everything that I seem to break. But all this framing leads to more banging and fixing, which eventually or maybe inevitably leads me to drywalling, painting, and finally designing and finishing people's rooms. For a living!

This is cool because now we're on the chapter talking about rooms.

Sometimes I find it amazing how people get so excited to let me design and create something special in their room. I mean, it's crazy. Your room is so personal, so the idea of someone else doing it for you seems so foreign, so unnatural. Now that being said, I may feel that way because someone once did try to redesign the room my brother and I shared.

During my childhood, we move from Atlanta to Oklahoma for a year so my dad can pass this hard legal class to be a lawyer, aka musician. While we were out (which is actually the title of another show I've worked on), my stepgrandmother decides to give us a special room to share. She's a beautiful woman from the old Hollywood era via Sarasota, Florida, and she has a passion for being crafty, as well as for enjoying a libation or two during the process. It must take her week upon week to create something both patriotic, chaotic, symbolic, and, well, almost demonic. I truly understand how the couples on *Trading Spaces* feel after I witness quite the transformation in our space. She must really be into the '70s-striped craze going on in fashion, because she creates a red, white, and blue vertical-striped room. Well, let's just call it what it really has become—a patriotic jail cell with bold, then thin, and then more BOLD stripes.

Not just on the walls. Oh no. It also has matching striped bedding, with matching color schemes, as well as matching trash cans that have been turned into Uncle Sam or a nutcracker or a combo of both.

My brother and I cry every night we're away from our childhood home, waiting to get back to Atlanta. However, now we're crying for another reason. I mean, we hated sharing the room already, but who wants to share Uncle Sam's prison cell when you're ten? The crazy part is that our stepgrandmother is so pleased with it. Now come to think of it, this is the payback that pays it forward to when I won't stop Hildi or any other designer from creating their own chaos in an unsuspecting person's room. But Lord . . . those people are adults who can afford to change it—come on; we're just kids. Family. The gift you can't give away. Or get rid of. Especially when they're full of gifts.

"FIVE TO ONE"

Day Five of writing.

"Five to one, baby; one in five. No one here gets out alive."

Sorry. I'll turn down the stereo.

Whooooooo. I sure do love trying to do the impossible. So these little tidbits are being written in the back of taxis and on airplanes or in someone's bathroom or garage or on the set of a design show. Because, well, we have to finish this thing in a week. The reason is to really put you, the beautiful reader, in the mind-set of what it's like living and pushing things to the extreme. It creates a chaotic environment. Which clearly is where I do my best work.

Look, I'll take on any cool new projects I've never done. I love going down avenues I've never traveled down before, not knowing if I'll do well but enjoying the idea of learning something new and experimenting with a new medium. As I've said, I've spent my whole life convincing people I can do things when I don't really know if I can do it. So why would I stop doing that now? Except for brain surgery. *No, Doc. You should keep the scalpel yourself. Let me just hold the light.*

It's about inspiration, about perspiration, about satisfaction. As an artist, I don't think you can ever be satisfied because you're always trying to outdo your last work. But it's also like they're selfies snapped in the moment.

People will ask me, "Why don't you have tattoos? You seem like a cool person who'd have them."

I tell them I don't like my old work. I wouldn't want to see something I put on my body ten years ago. *Oh dear heavens, I'm not doing that phase anymore. I'm out of that mood. That tat looks like I was out of my mind!*

I once do an art show in the '90s in Atlanta, showing off a bunch of graphic logos, things like grenades and symbols of the earth with the pin at the top. I have lots of interesting stuff, like a female alligator with sixteen bosoms that represents my mom. Another is a womb that has a power box in it. Great stuff like that. I remember a couple of guys telling me it's really cool stuff and asking if they can get tattoos of my artwork.

"You want to put that on your body for the rest of your life? Have at it!"

Art is about the moment and the mood, not about memorializing. It's about the great unknown. I'm always hoping I'll outdo myself and be amazed at what comes out. I love leaning in to the steering wheel and pushing the gas pedal, not pausing to look back in the rearview mirror. The former is finishing a room on *Trading Spaces* or *Extreme*; the latter is going back home to Mom's house and seeing an illustration you did in high school.

"Dear God, can you please take that down, Mom?"

"I'm really proud of it."

I don't think any true artist is ever satisfied. Everybody wants to continue to turn the page. I hope you want to keep turning these pages too. But that means I have to keep writing them, right?

What I'm trying to say, even though I'm not quite sure how I even got to this observation, is that no matter how exciting the book of life you're living is, there's always a chapter that's unexpected. That's why we have ups and downs, and why we have surprising things that thrill us or break our hearts.

For me, the ultimate thrill is the moment I'm in the middle of a project like this. Or in the middle of three of them. It's perhaps one of the only times I feel true elation, when I feel stoked and pumped. It's knowing something is coming together. And then you realize something else is coming down the road that's going to be arriving in two days.

The problem with ADHD is that people would love for you to start and FINISH a project. As you know, what you do is start one and then realize in the middle that you have to do another one. Then you find another project you never finished and suddenly you're doing three projects and none of them get finished.

No, that's not my subtle message to my editor. There are ways talented people can actually complete all three things at the same time. Sure, sometimes projects stay in limbo for a while. Sometimes they're dying a slow death in focus groups or in my unopened email from five years ago. But then when they're all a go and I'm working on them, people look at me and are like, "Are you out of your mind, Ty? Look at the chaos you're living in. This isn't healthy."

I'm fully aware of this. But I tell them I just have to finish these projects and then I'll get back to being healthy. But then something else will suddenly pop up.

I better keep going. Wait . . . what day is it again?

"IN YOUR ROOM"

If I had to add up the number of rooms I've designed on television, whether it's the furniture, wallpaper, fabric, artwork, or everything in the room, I would lose count. I mean, this is crazy, but not only have I been in your living room on television, but it's possible I was in your actual living room, or at least you know someone who knows someone who worked with me on a project in your town or neighborhood. Seriously, go ask. I'll wait . . . I mean, I've built furniture in your sister-in-law's cousin's cul-de-sac down the block. I've helped stick hay on walls or plastic flowers in bathrooms, not to mention installing all these heavy items usually made out of medium-density fibreboard (MDF) on walls and ceilings all over America. All on a show that changed the whole DIY landscape. Who saw that coming? I certainly didn't.

The moment the camera guy starts laughing and shaking the camera because he knows I'm measuring designer Frank for a coffin, especially since he already has the flowers—I guess that's what you call chemistry. On camera and off, we get each other's humor. And when Frank laughs hard, he looks like he's dying, which is even funnier.

So I'm guessing the TLC Network doesn't hire me for my carpentry skills but more likely for my people skills. I guess I either read people pretty well, or I let them read me (like you're doing now) enough that they feel comfortable being REAL with me. And in reality TV, that's always what's appealing. You know—those REAL moments. Like when I have a confrontational convo with Doug, and you can tell that . . . well, sometimes he's a real . . . well, you know what. So yeah, those are REAL moments. Actually, the entire cast of *TS* is incredibly real. Everyone is so different. They have different personalities and design styles. In fact, we're all still that way. It's like reaching into a variety pack of talent and ideas—you never know what you're going to get.

The other real moments are me pulling my hair out or beating my head against a table because I have seven projects or pieces of furniture to design and build in basically twenty-four hours. Oh yeah, right after the designers say, "By the way, I only have $38 dollars left for materials." Good times. Actually, the best of times. I guess I love a challenge, since I almost always say yes.

"I'll find a way."

That's my mantra, my method, my madness. Sometimes the frustration of completing all that work will lead to something being amusing, but not everything's always so amusing. It's stressful, especially because I want to show the designers and the world that I'm good at what I do—creating things. I don't even think the network knows I actually specialize in building furniture. Well, on *Trading Spaces* you can't always call it "high-end" furniture; you can call it low-cost and finished furniture.

The homeowners on *Trading Spaces* learn by doing, but they aren't the only ones. I am quickly learning a bit of everything. I learn how to build cheaply and quickly, how to create informative but also entertaining scenes, all while not cutting off any of my digits on the chop saw. I become a designing and building machine, working almost nonstop. Once I get in a rhythm, I'm not only good; I want to be better. It's such a rush to realize you're talented enough to show everyone just how good you can be. So you keep trying to outdo yourself if the designers leave enough money in their budget. I build sofas, solid wood beds out of Brazilian cherry. I mean, I build REAL nice furniture. Pretty soon, I want to prove that my design skills are just as good as my building skills. But the network wants to keep me, well, in the same box. Even though I'm already thinking outside it.

Here's the thing about being boxed in. Eventually you have to find a way to get out. Sometimes you can't wait for a door to open; sometimes you gotta build that door yourself. Sometimes you'll have to draw a line in the sand, and no, that's not a mixed metaphor. Not when you're on *Trading Spaces*, and the sand is literally in the room!

Sometimes you can't wait for a door to open; sometimes you gotta build that door yourself. Sometimes you gotta break out of the room you've built for yourself.

Sometimes you gotta break out of the room you've built for yourself. Then again, sometimes you're kicked out of it, like my mom and dad decide to do when they finally grow sick of me living with them while I'm in college. My mom will write me a note basically saying something like this:

> I'm afraid you are not respecting our rules. Our agreement was you can stay in this house as long as you have a job and are attending college, but your recent actions prove neither of those seem important to you.

They're leaving for the weekend and ask that I find another place to live by Monday. I have $22 to my name, but I decide to throw myself a going-away party. I run a hose from the hot water line going to the washing machine out to the outside deck to fill up a kiddie pool. Basically I pull a MacGyver move to create a makeshift hot tub.

Let's just say I go out with a bang . . . and no, I didn't blow anything up.

"SOMEBODY TOLD ME"

There are two things people often will say to me. The first is especially gratifying, especially since I'll always be that kid in the class causing chaos. I love it when parents of kids with ADHD or simply people who have creative, nutty children come up to me to say I'm an inspiration.

"My kid loves you! If *you* can make it, maybe he can."

After saying thanks, I'll always be honest with them.

"Yeah, but I got *really* lucky. Being in the right place at the right time with a TV show looking for someone with my skills. Skills I didn't even know I had!"

I never realized I'd be such a natural at this.

This ties in with the other thing I'm often asked: "Did you ever think about acting?"

Of course I have. The truth I've come to realize is that's what I've been doing ever since getting on television. But let me explain by telling you one of my favorite stories about pursuing an "acting career."

So in the '80s I do a bunch of commercials, but I'm not doing television every day, so I have no idea how I'll be behind a camera. I assume I'd be decent. I lived in New York back then, and I'm working with a men's modeling agency, which is run by a German woman named Renada. She knows I'm not the typical model since I don't trust anybody, nor do I really care about this industry. I'm making a living but don't really care whether I'm handsome or not. She knows my mentality is basically, *There's gotta be more to life than standing there looking like I'm smoking a cigar.* So one day, Renada reaches out to do me a favor.

"Look, Ty, I don't do this often. There's a guy I think you should meet. He's an acting teacher. He normally doesn't take models, but you seem to have something not a lot of people have."

This is extremely generous of her. Perhaps she's noticing something since I've landed four commercials in a row. So Renada takes me to the acting studio, where I go in and observe for a couple of classes. Eventually I'm able to introduce myself to the class. Of course, as soon as I start, I begin to act funny until the teacher interrupts me and the laughter of the class.

"Stop. Right now. Don't laugh at this show he's been putting on his whole life."

The room drops into deathly silence as this Cecil B. DeMille of acting coaches strides up to me.

"Look, buddy. You need to understand how important this is to all these people. I'm sure you've been a comedian your whole life, and that's fine, but we don't need this little show you're putting on."

I'm a bit stunned.

What are you—the father I just thought I ran away from?

"These are *professional* actors. They've made sacrifices to study this art. So if you're not serious about this, you need to leave the room."

I can't believe the gall of this guy.

"I'm just introducing myself. This is how I talk."

Later as I start to do a scene with a girl, I say the lines as if I'm basically reading them. I've never "acted" and I'm not an "actor" and I've never trained with "professionals" and I hate being around people who need quotation marks around them to signify their arrogance. Once again, the teacher barks at me and stops me cold.

"That's not it. You know what? You don't have the talent to be in this room. I should have known."

Now I'm not just ticked off, but I'm insulted. So I get angry and tell him off. Then he says, "That's it. Now say the lines." I say each word but imagine my hands around the teacher's neck, choking him while I'm uttering some stupid words from a screenplay. When I'm done, the man's expression has changed.

"Wow," he says, "now *that's* acting."

I know I've nailed the scene, but really, all I want to do is drive a nail into this guy's skull. I take the script, wad it up, and throw it at him. I walk to the door and then stop and turn around.

"Look, man, I don't know what your other job is, but clearly here you're a psychotherapist who uses acting to mess with people's minds. I get it. But if this is what acting is—where you tell me my issues and that you're a superior being—you can go to hell. I don't need this."

This guy isn't interested in teaching me. All he wants to do is break me.

When I tell my roommate in New York what happens, he shrugs it off. Dino's this tall and handsome guy who's half Indian and half Italian. His idol is Robert De Niro, and he spends a lot of time looking in the mirror and saying, "You talkin' to me?"

"You don't need acting class," Dino tells me. "You just need auditions."

"No. If I'm going to go down an avenue, I want to be the best at it."

I realize that acting is interesting, but will I ever be better than Sean Penn and Robert De Niro? Acting is being the most comfortable and natural person you can be in a given role. Yet the greats are on another level. They'll change their body weight and hair, put on makeup, and wear plastic noses. I'll see these types of actors and think, *Now, that's good acting*.

I assume I have the skills to do fairly well, but I'd probably be the Ty Pennington version of whatever character I'm playing. I know I'm never going to be amazing, so why even go down that road? It's the same conclusion I arrive at in my modeling career (after the Jeep goes off the road).

So here's the thing about being on television on reality shows: you're doing a more amplified version of yourself. I'm not talking about some of the shows that are scripted and basically excuses to act silly or eat pasta while talking about yourself. I'm talking about *Trading Spaces* and *Extreme*. I think I should answer this question in a different way: "Have you ever thought about acting?"

"Isn't that what I'm doing every day?"

There are times on *TS* and *Extreme* when I'm so exhausted and not in the mood to do anything other than sleep. After filming they'll come to me with the truth. "Ty, we can't use that shot. You look tired. We need that other guy, the funny, zany Ty."

"Oh yeah? Well that other guy is off work because he's resting somewhere."

So I have to bring back the amplified, energetic Ty. It doesn't matter what mood I'm in. For the shows, I'm supposed to be *that* guy all the time. For the comedic roles I'm playing, I imagine an actor who's going through divorce but who has to snap out of it. So yeah, I probably *am* an actor.

Here's another interesting thought. On *Extreme*, those tears I'm crying are real. If you study the method of acting, you're crying about something that really happened. So you know what? I guess I'm a REAL actor. A good one too, since a good actor is honestly just playing themselves—only it's a slightly modified version of that, which I think I kind of do every day.

I can't wait to see what the next character is going to be in the future. He's probably going to be limping a bit . . .

Here's what I know about the whole acting subject. I don't know if I'm a great actor, but I do know I'm better than some of the other "actors" I end up working with on TV. A couple of people end up overacting. For instance, I'll see people talking to a child we're designing a room for, and they suddenly go into William Shatner mode:

"So. Joey. Tell me. What would you like. To see. In your. Room?"

I try to intervene.

"Listen, Shatner. Why don't you just go, 'Hey, Joey,' instead of 'Tell me about what makes you tick'? You're scaring the child!"

I find it interesting to see the people on reality TV who are failed actors. I never wanted to be an actor. I just wanted to be myself and build stuff on TV. While never pursuing acting, suddenly I'm crying on camera and then laughing and going nuts. Maybe I'm going through all the phases of emotions that actors go through. Aren't the two symbols of acting the happy face and the sad face? That's exactly what I am on TV—one minute I'm sad, the next minute I'm happy.

Here's the irony—a lot of people on reality TV wanted to be actors but failed. I failed at so many things in life and end up being in a dramatic role like *Extreme* on reality TV. There should be an award for this: "And the Emmy for playing the dramatic role on reality TV goes to . . . Ty Pennington!"

Drama is part of the chaos of my life. And yes, drama is definitely a part of what I do on TV. But the drama you see is real—sometimes *too* real.

"AMERICAN IDIOT"

Back to *Trading Spaces* and my journey off that show and onto an even bigger one.

Once I get on television and know I'm able to make people feel comfortable on camera, I really try to become creative with the moments I have while being the American Handy Andy. There's no script on *Trading Spaces*, and this is one of the reasons I love it.

"Hey, Ty. So we have three minutes with you. Any ideas on what we can do that'll be interesting? We're trying to do an open, and we'll be in Florida. There will be a swimming pool. Swamp. Gator. Any ideas?"

In 2.5 seconds, I say, "Yes! Bring me a whole raw chicken. I need thirty feet of rope and a hook. And bring two drills."

The producer hugs me. "I love you." She doesn't even know what my idea is.

For this particular scene, I hook the chicken on a rope, start to lasso it, and act like I'm swinging it to catch a gator in the swamp. Hildi and Vern are nearby being filmed, so while I'm slinging this raw chicken, chunks of it begin flying at them and hitting their faces. Then in a miraculous moment, Hildi takes a drill and spears the chicken in midair. Suddenly blood and chicken juice go everywhere. I buckle over in laughter.

"Did you plan that?" the producer asks me.

"No way," I say. "You can't write this stuff."

This gives me more opportunities to plan comedy bits like this on *TS*. I'm suddenly given free rein, which is scary if you're giving it to me. And speaking of scary, one idea I have is doing this parody of *The Blair Witch Project*, with me running around holding a camera.

Wait . . . Isn't that what I end up doing on Extreme? *Interesting . . .*

I realize on *TS*—okay, as a carpenter, I know the camera's not going to be on me all the time. I know they'll come out to film me three or four times. So I need to be ready to be funny and kind of stupid. Which is awesome since I've been doing little stupid bits for friends and family all my life. So now I get to do it on regular TV. This will open up a whole new creative door.

The problem on *TS* is that it ends up getting a little campy near the end. And everybody starts to be the comedian. That's a problem, because in comedy, you have to have the funny guy and then the straight guy. That's why acts like the Smothers Brothers and Dean Martin and Jerry Lewis were so good. You need the idiot and the person unaffected by their humor. When everybody's trying to crack jokes, as it got to be on *Trading Spaces*, it can be too much. And for me to have to turn off jokes . . . well, that's just plain awkward since I've always been the loud, obnoxious, and over-the-top idiot on the show.

Oh, we have some really fun moments. It's amazing we're paid to come up with all these unique ideas. For instance, since Hildi is always wearing high heels, I make a bet with her that if I beat her in a race while running in heels, she will have to drop one of the jobs she has for me. So there we are on the front lawn, running in heels. I realize I might snap my ankle or something. Naturally, Hildi wins.

The show becomes an exercise in a creative class.

"Hey, what if we shoot me shoving my head in a watermelon while I'm having a conversation with Paige about how much I love fruit."

"Sure!"

How cool is that?

My whole life boils down to the fact that I've been entertaining people in one way or another. Like in the classroom. While I'm failing at all those classes, I'm laying the groundwork for a career that pays so much better than just art history. Well, a career that eventually will. I'm entertaining not just twenty pupils in a classroom but twenty million across the globe.

The idea of creating chaos is exactly why I'm hired to do what I do. "Bring me chicken and rope!"

So like I said earlier, when a parent tells me I'm an inspiration to their chaotic kid, I also tell them there's sheer luck involved when it comes to being in my industry. My role on *Trading Spaces* comes along right at the moment when TV is suddenly a new art medium, one where I can be this complete imbecile and use the physical comedy I've been performing my whole life. I'm literally doing a meshing of all the things I love to do. Building cool stuff. Creating stupid and silly home videos, but making it for a TV show. And seeing how a room is transformed in three days.

How awesome is that?

So then why in the world do I leave *Trading Spaces*?

"YOU NEVER GIVE ME YOUR MONEY"

By Day Five on *Extreme*, you're getting down to crunch time. So you have to be honest and come clean with the project. So I may as well come clean with you too. Especially since you've read this far. Eventually I have to come clean with the producers of *Trading Spaces*. Especially when I take a step back and see the reality of everything.

I'm on this groundbreaking show that changes the face of DIY shows. And I'm doing what I'm born to do, doing stuff I love to do. The show is popular, and I've suddenly become a celebrity. All this is great, and I'm living the dream, with the perfect job and fame and for—oh, wait, I'm still broke. And when I say *broke*, I'm quickly becoming financially *worse off* than I was before they called me.

I'm not sure what the designers are getting paid, but basically I'm being paid about $1,000 per episode on *TS*. Yes, that's one thousand dollars per episode of this tremendously successful, genre-breaking television series. A grand for three days of hard work. Professionals doing the same amount of work are getting a lot more money.

Think of how I feel in 2002 when I still owe the IRS my first two children and I'm shopping for groceries. I'm buying a loaf of bread and some beans to save money, and as I go through the checkout aisle, I see a magazine announcing that the cast members of *Friends* are making a million dollars. EACH OF THEM. MAKING A MILLION DOLLARS. PER EPISODE. Then I think of my last check that hovered right around $1,000.

I'm not a guy working at a Jack in the Box, frustrated by the young, good-looking cast members of this popular television show. I'm young! And I'm on one of the most popular television shows around! Come on!

Then it's confirmed that I'm soooo hot. *People* ends up choosing me as one of the hottest or hunkiest or whatever-it's-called guys of the year. A photographer comes down from Tennessee to take pictures of me on the couch sitting on my porch. Sure, I'm probably at the bottom of their list of sexiest men, but still—I'm on the hot list and I'm only being paid $1,000. Seriously? I'm worth at least $2,000 an episode, right?

I end up going to Leigh, the producer who hired me.

"Come on, Leigh! I can't survive on this."

The reality is I'm gone for two weeks and then home for another two weeks.

"I can't start another job when I get home because I have to turn around and leave. So you guys have become my only income. That means I'm making $2,000, maybe $3,000 a month! I'm barely surviving. Look, what if they pay me on a different show as a carpenter? Why can't I do another show?"

"That's not my call."

"Leigh, seriously—I can't do this!"

While I'm yelling and trying to act like a dominant male, she gets up quietly and shuts the door to her office.

"Now if you want to talk about this reasonably, we can sit down and talk about it," she says.

"Okay. I'm sorry for yelling, but I'm desperate. I'm like in major debt. I have to pay bills. I'm never home. They don't pay me enough to do this show."

She reminds me of the obvious. "None of us are getting paid what we want. But realize this is probably a stepping-stone to something bigger."

"Yeah, a stepping-stone I'm going to have to lay myself at three or four in the morning to get there."

"That's possible, but either way, it's a stepping-stone. You don't know what the future has in store. Remember—two years ago people didn't even know your name."

"Yeah, I see your point, but . . ."

So I ask the people in charge to put me on another show. They have another one called *While You Were Out*, and let's just be honest—they've ended up putting out three different copies of *Trading Spaces*. But I don't want to do *Trading Spaces, Family Version*. That's crazy. I'm not going to be the guy who takes out an eye with a nail gun because somebody thinks it's cool to put tools in kids' hands! The show, however, doesn't want me going anywhere else.

"We really like you where you are."

"You guys are really tying my hands," I tell them.

To make ends meet, I start booking home shows and appearances, and I end up making more doing this than I'm making on the show itself. I'm doing so many that *TS* will call me at times, and I'll tell them, "Sorry, I'm already booked this weekend." The show gets smart and ends up making a Ty Pennington clause: all bookings have to go through them. That just shows you how quickly *Trading Spaces* got successful. Back then, they didn't expect us to become so popular that we could end up getting bookings like this off the show.

Leigh was right. The show is indeed a stepping-stone. And I'm able to do enough things to keep the lights on. Sure, there starts to be a little resentment from the higher-ups, but it's not like I didn't ask them to let me work on something else. It's not like I'm looking a gift horse in the mouth. It's just that, well, the horse is really me! And I'm a rider and I like to run fast, so I'm going to run and make sure I'm going to run wherever the fields are green. If you're going to leave me in the field gnawing on the same old hay, then you're not going to get the best out of me.

Three years after the show launches, I decide that it's time to exit. This third season, they decide to go from $1,000 to actually spending

$100,000 on one special episode. I'm thinking, *You won't pay your people, but you're going to spend this much for a room? What—are you going to do it all in gold?* After being refused a decent raise or even a separate show to make a little more income, I take the biggest risk of my life—walking away from the greatest job I'd ever been given. A job like that only comes along once in a lifetime.

Wait . . . Come to think of it, make that twice in a lifetime. *Hello, reboot.*

So there I am, homeless and looking for a place in California, and soon to be jobless once I finish my final season on *Trading Spaces.* You know, you hear all these words of advice, like "When a door of opportunity opens, go through it." The truth is sometimes there is no door of opportunity. The one you came through a moment ago slams shut, and now it's just an empty room full of walls.

There I am, staring at the walls in a tiny one-room apartment in Venice, California.

What'd I just do? I walked away from the best job ever.

I'm reminded my whole life has been rooms full of walls. Now I'm kicking myself and the walls. It's actually hard to kick yourself, but I figure out how.

I learn something during this time: while you're being patient and waiting on another door to open, quit whining and start beating on doors, even if you don't know the person who lives there. After all, this is how I used to drum up work as a handyman. But if you really want to beat down a door, I suggest you do it with a sledgehammer. It feels amazing and has a lasting impact. Besides, who needs doors when you want to be seen by as many viewers as possible?

I say go big. No, I say go extremely big. And this is exactly where I go.

Frank is one of the few people on *Trading Spaces* that I tell I'm leaving. It's on my last episode. We're filming in Chicago. Some great things are happening at this time, like Sears signing me to work with them. We're on the campus of Northwestern, and Frank gives me a big hug with tears in his eyes.

"There are rare people you meet in life," Frank says. "You're one of the most talented people I've ever met, and I've met a lot of people. But you've got that 'it.' You go out there and you live your life. We were blessed to have you on the show."

I can't believe this. Now I'm getting all emotional too.

"So help me God, Frank—if you make me cry, I'll kill you!"

He's such an awesome human being. So genuine. All of them are this big family that I'm leaving. But if I don't make this decision, another door won't open. It feels like a year, but it's really only two or three months before the opportunity with *Extreme Makeover: Home Edition* comes along. (And if you need a refresher, go back to page 25 and read the "Magic Bus" section.)

It's interesting and ironic that on *TS* I'm starting to feel stifled and I'm jealous that I'm not designing rooms. So along comes a job where I get to design the room and finally be creative.

Here's a lesson in life: in the creative industry, people constantly move because change is the best thing for ideas. It can come from a new environment, a new desk, a new coworker, or all of the above. I know I've done everything I could on *Trading Spaces*. It's time to go down another road.

"WHOLE LOTTA LOVE"

Let's face it, it's no secret that I want to be more of a designer than just a carpenter who builds boxes out of MDF (that'd be medium-density fibreboard). It's also no secret that cutting MDF all day will leave your skin and nostrils full of a fine brown dust, a kind that's so appealing to hear being hacked up in the bathroom or during a dinner. Truly lovely. However, the leftover paste can work really well as hair-sculpting gel. Fact.

Okay, so where was I? Yes, it's also no secret that I've just left the best job I've ever been given. Now I'm afraid my name's going to become dusty, stored away on a shelf that I myself most likely built. That door I'm speaking about is the door to *Extreme Makeover: Home Edition*.

Lucky for me, the door of opportunity opens long enough for me to sneak in and lock it behind me. That's when I discover another door, one that the producers and I start talking about from the get-go. I'm talking about the door to my "secret room," which becomes a major feature in every episode of *Extreme*.

Honestly, I'm incredibly surprised by what the producers will say: "We know you want to design more, so the other designers will work on the kitchen, living room, and all the other house stuff, but you will have a special SECRET room you design for the hero of the story. We won't see it until the very end—to give us that big surprise reveal."

Now remember, this is all said *before* we even start filming the first episode.

You need to understand what this means. For me, hearing this is like winning the lottery. Not only do I now have a new job, but it looks like I'll be able pour my heart into a cool project that will have significant meaning. Even better than that, it will be a secret throughout the entire building process, so no one will see it until the house and the room are finished.

By the way, it's hard to keep an entire room a secret from everyone. But it's totally worth it. This turns out to be a good thing for so many reasons:

1. It allows me to work without any critique or input. And trust me, the other designers are not only as competitive as I am, but also just as dry and sarcastic. So a private secret room to work in is a major plus.
2. It really pushes me to go even more EXTREME, since revealing the room always comes as the grand finale of the episode.
3. In television, it not only adds a little mystery, but it also sometimes

hides the drama instead of showcasing it. Especially when something goes wrong, but also when I'm *literally* in another secret location, in another secret room, in another secret state, filming a second secret show with another secret film crew called Team Bravo, aka the B team. (More on that later.)

—————

The fact that we already have this secret room in the story arc of the show is such a blessing since you never get to see what's going on behind the closed door. There's always something going on, especially when communication becomes more difficult when you (the designer) aren't on the job site.

For example, wallpaper should be something that can easily go up without me being there to help. In one episode of *Extreme*, however, it will end up being applied upside down. In hindsight, this is easy to do since this is custom wallpaper I designed on the computer to look like enormous hanging vines. The plan is to get these little monkeys to hang from the ceiling like a mobile for this little kid's room (think Barrel of Monkeys). I'm obviously going for a jungle theme.

Literally an hour before the family gets back home, with all the chaos and craziness in the house, I walk in on my team frantically trying to assemble the monkeys tail-to-tail. I notice the mistake immediately.

"Wow . . ." I say, taking it all in and laughing. "This looks amazing. I wasn't sure if the wallpaper would work, but it totally does. Even though it's upside down. Ha!"

When I see the looks of disappointment on my teammates' faces—they're so afraid to let me down—I feel bad and realize that no matter how the room turns out, I'll always have to tell them it's awesome. Because honestly, it *is*, considering what was there before. They're just so freaked out because they know I'm a perfectionist. Just like I did in art school, I always have a plan A, plan B, and a plan C. Something inevitably is going to fail or not show or just go horribly wrong. The great news about this is you will most likely never know because the room is a SECRET. Get it?

The rooms I will end up designing on *Extreme* will be totally different animals than the rooms on *Trading Spaces*. They'll really focus on a special person, so the room will need to just blow their minds and really be a dream come true. When it comes to designing the furniture, wall treatments, lighting, and all of the above, I pull out all the stops to make it the best room I've ever done.

I end up designing and building this one bed to look like a cross between a camper and a cabin. It's like a modern camping module, elevated off the floor so you step up into it when you want to lie down for the night. This room is for a kid who is so sick that he has to spend most of his time inside. Since he loves being outside, especially camping, I transform the walls into a mountain forest with a custom mural that's so lifelike it feels like you're camping in Yellowstone National Park. Not only is the room transformed, but the bed no longer even looks like a bed. It's become a camper. And yes, we even make the ceiling glow so he can sleep under the stars at night. This type of creative work becomes so much fun.

I have to admit that I love doing kids' rooms. Maybe it's because I've always been a kid myself, or it's because of the horror I was left with after my grandmother designed my room. Remember the vertical stripes? That's hard to forget. Come to think of it, I sort of specialize in bedrooms, and I've designed lots of beds. In fact, a cameraman friend will notice this fact too one day.

"Do you ever think about how many babies have been made in all the beds you've designed and built?" he asks me.

"Well, no, I hadn't. Until *now*. And I'm pretty sure that's all I'll think about from now on. Thanks for that."

The truth is that I've put a lot of love into making those beds, so it makes sense that a whole lotta love will be made in them. Ha! Now that being said, not all beds I design are beautiful, ornate adult beds made out of hard woods like walnut with intricate cutouts on the headboards that give them a very rich finish. Of course, I don't just build a stand-alone bed. I always make sure it has other pieces, like bedside tables or even a credenza or bench to match.

Sometimes you not only create something beautiful, but you surprise yourself by designing something so unique that it's a breakthrough. It becomes something you're so proud of because it's never existed before you created it.

One of those eureka moments is when I design a room for a little girl who's fighting a disease that forces her to stay indoors where her body has a better chance of fighting infections and staying healthy. She really loves flowers and the idea of being outdoors, so I design a room that looks like she lives in a flower garden. I make large wooden stencils to paint gigantic, bold, colorful flowers on her walls as well as huge flowerpots hanging in the inside of her windows. In order for her to really feel the grass on her bare feet, we install wall-to-wall artificial turf that looks and feels so incredibly real. But I'll save the best for last.

Like I said, sometimes you get an idea so good you surprise even yourself.

This one comes to me in a sketch for what I want her bed to look like. I illustrate the side tables that I want to be able to flip down out of the headboard and sort of float out of where it's cut out in the shape of an oval. Those ovals will have clip-on lights above them that resemble antennas. Of course,  the ovals will look like eyes. As I start sketching more, creating supports that look like cricket legs and wing shapes for the platforms, the bed starts to come to life. Once the sketch is complete, there it is—something I call the Bed Bug. A bed that looks like a large, friendly bug sitting on the lawn in your flower garden room. The oval eyeball side tables really give it that happy grasshopper kind of feel. And it can all be made out of two sheets of plywood and fit together like puzzle pieces. It's one of those "wow, this is a really great design" moments.

There are lots of great ideas that happen behind the door of Ty's secret room, but some really make me incredibly happy because I know we've made something truly unique and special. Let's face it, I like to stand out a little bit, and I think great design should do the same. Not to the point that it's loud and annoying, like someone screaming at you with a megaphone, but I think you know what I mean.

Can you hear me now?!

Day

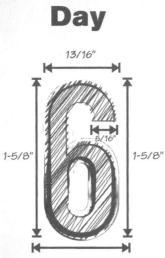

LOVE AND
COMMUNITY

Love and Community

Love and pain—they're always extreme.

I think sometimes what we do in life is a reflection of so many aspects of our own lives. When I look back at an episode of *Extreme*, the first thing that jumps out at me is the story. Not just the story of the deserving family, but the entire story from start to finish. It seems to mimic, in my opinion, life itself. It starts out very serious, where the situation is unstable and the outcome is uncertain. Then the narrative comes to life like a newborn. First with screams of surprise followed by tears and then replaced with laughter. This is what I mean: the show is sort of a reflection of life, bringing you up and down like a roller coaster. One minute we're sobbing while seeing how tough the twists and turns can be; the next minute we're screaming with joy and excitement while destroying every obstacle in sight. Ultimately what we're experiencing is the fine line between love and pain that can bounce like the little ball in a pinball machine.

I wonder sometimes if I'm lucky to end up as the leader and the narrator of this extreme example of reality, or if it's simply fate. I may never know the answer, but what I do know is that everything in life is uncertain, and it can all change in an instant. For the better and sometimes for the worse. Life has a really dark sense of humor; it seems to enjoy pointing out the irony in so many situations. We can all relate to others going through huge things both good and bad (and they're never just small things, right?).

One of the questions I'm always asked is how I handled hearing all those heartbreaking stories every week on *Extreme*. "It has to be hard, doesn't it?" Yeah, of course it's hard. It's absolutely gut-wrenching. You can't fully comprehend what a family is going through, but you can begin to imagine the pain of realizing what they've lost when they invite all of us into their home to share their story.

Every time, I end up asking myself the same sorts of questions: *How am I even qualified to try to comfort someone going through the most horrific thing you can think of? How am I qualified to tell them it's gonna be okay?*

Then I remind myself that I'm not. No one is qualified. But we've all had to be strong for a friend going through difficult times. You don't have all the answers, but you find ways to comfort them. You can show them it's hard now, but with time and help and the steady turning of the page, anybody can keep going and one day laugh again.

The irony is sometimes the person who is there for someone else, the one being strong, may also be going through a personal nightmare. But they know if they can help a person in need get through the rough and raging waters of life, then maybe they can learn how to get across them too. Maybe someone will in turn be there for them too.

You see, now by Day Six on *Extreme*, we're really to the HEART of the story. When I think back to all the moments on this show when we're changing the lives of deserving families forever, I don't just think about the family members themselves. I remember also the nameless volunteers in blue T-shirts, all who have their own stories to tell, who are going through their own pain, with losses and families of their own. Who put all that on hold to help another. I think about my team of coworkers who are away from their home and families for almost three hundred days out of the year. Think about that.

We used to say back at our hotel after finishing houses back-to-back in seven days, our behind-the-scenes documentary would be titled *Extreme Makeover Home Edition: Rebuilding Lives and Dreams for Deserving Families While Destroying Our Own*. Ha! The sad thing is, this is kind of true. We're all part of this crazy circus that builds homes but never gets to *go* home. We just keep going and going, catching a few hours of sleep in hotel rooms before we start the next project in the next town.

Only a few will last nine seasons of living like this. Not many can live the circus life as a performer. Honestly, not much of anything can last that long living like that. There are so many things you lose. First, well, your looks start to go because you're always so tired. Then pretty much everything else—your place, your friends, your girl. And if your pet is waiting on you, then they've surely left, along with leaving you a little surprise on the carpet before they depart.

To survive you have to have a strong family or a strong relationship with whomever is waiting for you back home. With people who believe that working like this is for a greater cause, who believe it's worth it. To be honest, the only time I've seen it work is when the wife just seems to say, "If you can't beat 'em, join 'em." This is exactly what happens when our project manager, Dave Bohler, is joined by his wife on our job site one day. You see—that's love. Sure enough, a year later, they have a baby.

As for my love life . . . for those waiting for me back home . . . I'm always on a building site, helping to construct a home for someone else. And when all the demolition is finally over and I'm back home and I see my own bus move . . .

Like I said, love and pain—they're always extreme.

"25 OR 6 TO 4"

Day Six of writing. Talk about love and pain.

Two days left. I hope you understand what kind of pressure I'm under to deliver an entertaining little read. It's gonna be great, I know this. I've already got the word count. Actually, I may have more than enough. Wait—does that mean I talk too much?

The bad news is I'm having a nightmare situation with a room I'm designing on the new *Trading Spaces* reboot. The room is almost as small as the window of time I have left on this book. So, okay, right—switching focus to the task at hand.

Time to take some multivitamins and multitask so I can multistep and get all this multimedia to the multitudes.

"CRAZY"

So there I am after quitting *Trading Spaces* and wondering what I've done. But honestly, things could have been worse. *Much* worse.

Around the second year of *TS*, I get a call from a producer. "We're about to shoot a show. About a single guy. We think you'd be a great candidate, and we'd love for you to be on the show. You'll be living in a house with twenty women. You get to go on dates with them and make out with them. Ultimately you'll make a decision to marry one."

Interesting concept that's never been done before. I call my buddy William out in LA and tell him about the show.

"Do it! Are you kidding me? That sounds fantastic."

Except there's one problem—my girlfriend. We're pretty serious, but still, I have to consider everything. Right?

"So let me run something by you. I'm guessing you won't be okay with this. But just for the sake of conversation."

Yeah, I don't end up choosing to do the show. Thank God, because instead of going on to be known as this compassionate and caring human on *Extreme*, I'd be one of those Deuce Bigalow guys on *The Bachelor*. It would have been the worst move of my life. No matter how you come out of it, that's how you're labeled. But at the time, who knew? I sure didn't.

When I first decide to work with Endemol, the production company that ends up producing *Extreme Makeover: Home Edition*, we initially will shoot a pilot for another brilliant show called *Exhausted*. Here's the premise: you keep people awake for three entire days. Basically it's *Fear Factor* with no sleep. I'm the host, so I'm trying to be funny in every scene, yet they're constantly telling me to stop. They basically want me to be Joe Rogan.

Imagine the show. People dressed in pajamas are forced to walk off the plank while being sprayed by a hose—stuff like that. You have to be the last man standing who's not asleep. The problem is everybody—and I mean everybody—begins to start falling over. Even the cameramen. The title of the show is perfect since I've never been more exhausted in my life. I finally realize this is insanity.

"If this is television, I don't want to be a part of it," I tell the producers.

The truth is, nobody wants to be a part of this. Thankfully, the next concept we work on is *Extreme*.

So let's talk about the name—*Extreme Makeover: Home Edition*. It's gotta be the worst name for a show ever. It's way too long and it contains a colon. (And no show should ever contain a word that refers to your large intestine.) The original name is *Space Invaders*, which I actually like better, but since ABC owns the rights to the *Extreme Makeover* brand, they think to simply come up with a home edition of it.

As I've said before, the original idea the agency packages together could have been so bad. They cast all these people together who they assume *won't* get along with each other, who they actually *want* to argue and experience angst. None of us know exactly what we have at the beginning of *Extreme*. We're basically trying to do *Trading Spaces* on steroids, building bigger projects with bigger emotions. I'm the guy at the start telling them I want to do a show for people to cry for all the right reasons.

When I start on *Extreme*, I'm coming off sleepless nights of questioning why I ever quit the best job I've ever been given and wondering if I've made the worst choice of my life. Most people on *Trading Spaces* feel as if I abandoned them, and many don't realize why. They don't know I want anything—*anything*—to help me pay off my debts. They also don't realize I asked for a little help from a show I helped gain the highest ratings on the planet.

When we see that first family's reaction on *Extreme*, when they walk *around* the bus (before we decide to move it) and when everybody has tears of emotion on their faces, I realize my own tears are partially coming from relief. This is our EUREKA! moment.

I'm not sure if people are going to like this, but by God, we need to do this again.

When the show airs, people don't just like *Extreme*; they love it.

If you watch the first season of *Extreme*, you'll see that my personality doesn't change much from *TS*. I'm me on both shows. The only difference is on one, I'm the guy running around with a megaphone acting berserk in the middle of an exploding house. Which brings me back to the kid with a megamouth acting berserk in the middle of an exploding classroom. Talk about the irony.

At the start of *Extreme*, as they prepare to shoot a scene, they try to get everybody to stop working.

"Hey, can you turn off the generators and the nail guns so we can hear Ty talk?"

I'm like, "No! Turn everything up to full volume. It's going to seem more dramatic if I'm screaming over the noise of a jackhammer!"

"I see your point," they'll say. "But it's going to be a nightmare for the editors."

"Then why did they get hired? That's exactly what their job is. To figure it out!"

I want to create as much noise and chaos as I can. That's more energetic and exciting, and that's why I'm here. I'm not hired to be someone like Richard Attenborough, talking with a calm and astute demeanor. "The following family has experienced calamity after calamity, and in tonight's episode, I will sit down with each of them while we watch the careful rebuilding of their house." Yeah, they didn't pick me for that. They picked me to be entertaining and obnoxious and fun and LOUD. So that's exactly what I'll be. For nine entire seasons.

I don't know if it's from my crazy childhood, but when there's chaos in a room, I have an ability to take it and focus. I literally become the eye of the story. In the center of the craziness, I can focus on what needs to be done. Sure, the hours are crazy and we're doing impossible things and people are breaking down because they're utterly fatigued and materials don't show up and literally everything can be going terribly wrong, yet in the center of it all is me. And I'm thriving.

"WE ARE FAMILY"

Day Six on *Extreme* is always intense, with the project finally nearing completion and an entire community gathering to work hard and show love to the family. By now the viewers have learned a lot about the family being helped. Not only that, but they've also learned more about all the designers on the show. They've bonded with them in the same way we all bond. But that initial bond doesn't happen on our first show. In fact, as we start to do more and more episodes, some of the designers initially become resentful toward me because I'm in, like, every scene. So when they see me, it's hard for them to be my best friends.

"Oh, hi, Pennington. What are they having you do today?"

"Sorry, guys, for your utter jadedness," I joke, knowing we have a big job to do.

What binds us together is not only the mission at hand but the amusement we find along the way.

I sort of rate how good of a friend someone might be by their laugh, and if it's a real, genuine laugh. You know the difference. For example, I once worked with Tim Gunn, and he was laughing so much he sounded as if he was vomiting. I'd never heard his infectious, hilarious laugh. It's just the greatest thing. If someone can just let go and laugh, I fall in love with them. Let's face it, laughter is the best medicine, especially on a show as heavy as *Extreme*.

The moment I truly bond with designer Tracy Hutson, who is this talented and funny woman who becomes kind of like my sister on the show, is when we're shooting a video in the middle of the desert in California. While we're there on this farm, with the family on vacation, we do a family check-in. They bring out a Shetland pony named Cherry Cola, and the horse is as high as my hips.

"She's a little spooky," the wrangler warns me. "Don't get too close."

This doesn't stop me. I climb on Cherry Cola with my camera and begin to film myself. But I'm still standing high enough that I'm not even touching the pony's back.

"Hey, family! We have all your friends here, including Cherry Cola!"

Just as I swing around, the Shetland pony freaks out and takes off galloping. As I'm being dragged across the farmland, Tracy's on the ground laughing so hard she's almost gagging. It's like we have to give her oxygen since she's cracking up so bad. The minute I see her overcome with hilarity like this, I can't help thinking, *Snot just flew out of your face. I'm going to be your friend. For life.* And sometimes laughter is the greatest gift you can receive.

Eventually the entire team will become close like this, communicating like siblings stuck on a family trip. Sometimes we can't help but crack up. We become so used to each other's company, we have to tease and make fun of each other. Like sometimes when I'm telling a family's situation while we're all in the bus, and we're trying to capture the raw emotion and power of the story while watching the tape that's been sent in.

"So, hey, guys. Look at this tape. We're going to have to help these guys. It's lucky we're here in time."

They become so used to hearing me say this that they'll sometimes make fun of my sincerity while I'm doing it.

"They don't need a new house. They need cleaning supplies!"

I'll always be like, "Sorry, yeah, we can't use that."

It's bad enough we have to live in that bus. Speaking of cleaning supplies, Paulie will wreck the toilet so many times we all literally have to evacuate the bus. We're physically and emotionally exhausted, and yet we still have jobs to do. So any moments of levity are appreciated.

"Look, guys," I'll sometimes tell the designers. "This show is different. It's about helping people. So as jaded and tired as you might be, we're going to go in and do some positive stuff."

OH ARE WE, TY?

I know I've found a family when the designers begin to mock me as much as my brother might. That's when you know you really are around special people.

"YOU MAKE ME FEEL GOOD"

"What's your favorite *Extreme Makeover: Home Edition* episode?"

This is another question I'm often asked, and I always have to put my favorites in different categories. I imagine it's like asking, "Which of your children do you love the most?" I love all the episodes, but of course I do have my favorites for different reasons.

There's my favorite room I've designed that's above and beyond anything else I've done. As always, it connects with the family story in an amazing way. For me, it's the room I design for the Kadzis family in Tallahassee, Florida. It's a heavy, heavy show. George and Barbara Kadzis have an incredible family with seven kids, six who are special needs children from China. George is battling brain cancer, and he literally goes into the hospital the night before we show up. The swelling in his brain has increased, and he's lost his eyesight.

The room I design is an insanely beautiful, Asian-inspired bedroom for George and Barbara. It blends the story of them adopting these children with the importance that music plays in all their lives. At the end, Stevie Wonder shows up and walks into the house to sit down at the piano and sing. Then, even more moving and surprising, he changes the song lyrics for "I Just Called to Say I Love You" just so we can actually use the song on the show. No artist does that without having to pay him!

Imagine the emotion the family has as he's singing the song and then changes the lyrics for George. "I am here because he loves you," Stevie sings to the family about George, who's in the hospital.

It's heartbreaking when we hear the news right after we leave this wonderful family. The show shares this with viewers: "Three days after getting their new home, George Kadzis lost his battle with cancer."

Another way I judge my favorite episodes is by measuring the impact the story has on me personally. One episode I'll never forget is with Boey Byers in Oregon, another person battling cancer. I'll share her story later in this chapter. I'll never forget this incredible young girl. Neither will my friend Michael Connelly, the assistant director for the show. He's a hard, rugged, and bearded Bostonian from the south side (I'm guessing). That little girl *slays* him.

So sometimes it's this work of art you've done that is so significant in someone else's life, and sometimes it's this little person who becomes so significant in your own life. I wrote a whole book about this, but it's true when I say that design can literally change your life.* When you meet someone who impacts you like this and when you design something you

---

* Ty Pennington, *Good Design Can Change Your Life: Beautiful Rooms, Inspiring Stories* (New York: Simon & Schuster, 2008).

know will light up their faces and their lives, it stays with you a long time. Even now, I remember moments with families like it happened just yesterday. The details are still all there.

Think about it. There's a huge difference between designing a room for a couple who need a taupe-colored bedroom and a couple going through something tragic and who need a new house because a plane crashed into their old one or it's full of poisonous gas. You're creating something for a reason, for a family and a community, and this very something is going to result in a nation full of viewers who will talk about it at their jobs on Monday mornings.

I remember hearing a fan talk about this once. "What I love about your show is that I feel good about going into work the next day and trying to do something positive and great in this world."

How many shows do THAT?

Instead of putting out hate, this show inspires love. And love is a beautiful, complex, and fascinating concept for me. It's one I'm still trying to figure out to this day.

"LOVE, REIGN O'ER ME"

My first experience with love is when I'm ten years old and standing at a bus stop. No, no, not that other time when I'm holding my soiled underwear in my hand. That's hard love. It's when I'm living in Oklahoma, and I'm standing next to a girl waiting for the bus, and suddenly I have this weird, tingling feeling inside me. I'm feeling warm, but it's not because of the jacket I'm wearing. I'm having the craziest, strangest thoughts ever.

Girls aren't so bad. Actually, they smell great!

Ever since this moment, I'll know girls are the best thing ever. I love them. Let's face it, women are *so much more* attractive than men (to me). I need to just give a big thumbs-up and a nice pat on the back to every woman ever born, because somehow and someway they will still decide to be with men and fall in love with us and make babies with us, even though we look like this. I mean, seriously. We're hairy and smelly and just . . . you know . . . Women don't wake up in the morning and think, *Yes! I can't live without THAT!*

What women desire is your essence. They fall for humor and for compassion and for wit and for you. So love and marriage and happily ever afters—that's what we all want, right? Or at least this is what we set out in life to try to find.

I've taken a different approach with this. Like everything in my life, things have been done a little differently. And since I hate even saying the L-word in a relationship because I believe it takes the essence of what it is out of the equation, I'll put together another playlist to sum up my thoughts and my history with this particular word:

1. **"LOVE STINKS" BY THE J. GEILS BAND.** To me, *love* is a four-letter word. And for me, it's spelled backward, and it's *EVOL*. I spend my whole life growing up in a family where I hear my parents arguing, so naturally I sorta assume that's what love is all about.

2. **"HOW DEEP IS YOUR LOVE" BY THE BEE GEES.** I never get the nerve to ask a girl to prom or a dance. Despite being the class clown, I'm actually shy when it comes to relationships. I will only go to one dance, and it's after a girl asks me. I remember it vividly because I borrow a van to take her. Somehow a friend of my mom's has this 1970s van with the stripe across the side and that weird bubble window on it. Everything inside is this gross shag carpet. I can only imagine what the parents think when I show up to pick up their daughter. Since this is seventh grade, I'm being driven by my mom's friend.

"Look, Fred. He's getting out of that van."

"Look, Susan. The driver's getting out too. Look at that shirt he's wearing!"

I'm sure they're just thrilled to be letting their daughter go to the dance with Ty and his hippie chauffeur.

3. **"LOVE WILL TEAR US APART" BY JOY DIVISION.** *Love* is a four-letter word, because sometimes you find it. But it's not the sort of fantasy love where you meet someone and you think, *This is what I've been waiting for all my life*. Instead, you realize when you're young that we always seem to fall for the wrong ones.

Case in point—while I'm in Japan living on ramen and rice with my modeling career, I go into a bar one night and see a girl laughing, dancing, and raising the roof. One minute she's raising hell on top of the bar; the next she gets hit in the head with a ceiling fan, so I dive to catch her so she doesn't split her skull open when hitting the concrete floor. (True story.) Naturally I've discovered my soulmate here. A stunt person—who's hilarious.

But soon I realize the truth.

Yo, I can't be here to save you! I'm looking for someone to save me!

I'm usually the person on the bar being hit with a ceiling fan.

Look, if this is going to work, you have to have my *back!*

The problem is when the person you fall in you-know-what with is actually a little wilder and worse off than you are. Sometimes they actually turn out to be the best and worst thing to come into your life at that point in time. Sometimes timing is everything.

"Good times, bad times. You know I've had my share."—Led Zeppelin

Moral of my story: we're either looking for something we can't have or running to something we most likely shouldn't be running to.

"Aging is an extraordinary process where you become the person you always should have been."—David Bowie

4. **"CRAZY LITTLE THING CALLED LOVE" BY QUEEN.** Life can be challenging when you have ADHD. On one side, there are responsibilities, like showing up on time for your job and not committing to too many things. But a lot of people forget that it takes a lot of skills to keep a relationship as well. It can be difficult to communicate clearly what you're feeling and doing, or what you want out of the relationship.

Two very distinct forces are working AGAINST any sort of relationship I might try to have with another:

1. ATTENTION (OR LACK OF). Even though I can hold the attention of others for quite some time, it's hard for me to keep my attention on one subject for more than a few minutes. And what do relationships and romance and LUV need? Attention.
2. DISORDER. This is exactly what I'm always creating. Absolute disorder. Which nobody wants for the rest of their lives, right?

Relationships can be tough. Imagine if the problem isn't just not knowing how your loved one feels. What happens when he can't even show up for a dinner or a date because he got distracted?

5. **"ALL MY LOVE" BY LED ZEPPELIN.** It's not like I don't try. Because sometimes when love comes to town, you just can't help it. Sometimes they can be your best friend, and they can be a perfect match.

The problem with me is that I overthink everything, questioning if I'm doing the right thing and if I should be doing this or that. I focus more on projects than people because that's always the happy place. People don't want to settle down with someone who's always unsettled himself. A woman doesn't want to journey along with a man who's constantly questioning if he's going down the right path.

The reason I'm probably not married is because I look at love like a room with windows and doors. If you screw the windows and nail the doors shut, I feel like I'm going to suffocate. I prefer to have the windows and doors open, so if someone wants to leave, they can any moment. The moment I'm locked in, I feel like I've become a prisoner.

That said, I've been in ten-year relationships and never hear the sirens of AC/DC's "Jailbreak."

I've decided that if I am ever going to be married, I'll do this: I'll take my bride-to-be up in a plane and then throw a parachute on the person who's looking at me and telling me they want to spend the rest of their life with me.

"Do you really want to do this?" I'll ask them.

If they say yes, I'll throw them out the window and then jump out myself. (Wait, maybe I should go first.) We can say our vows on the way down. If we don't die, then I guess we're stuck with it!

6.) "BIZARRE LOVE TRIANGLE" BY NEW ORDER, MIXED WITH "LOVE IS BLINDNESS" BY U2. She tells me over and over again, "You always have a project. The problem is I need a project."

So then she goes and finds her project. Well . . . it's more than that.

She has a baby. The only problem is, this isn't *your* baby; it's someone else's.

I don't need to explain how this can really put a damper on the whole notion of love.

Did I mention how I spell *love*?

7.) "LOVE TO BE LOVED" BY PETER GABRIEL. The people I work with who still manage to keep loved ones in their life—now those are my heroes. Because I do appreciate love. I've just learned that you have to remember others, that you have to show appreciation, that you have to not take for granted the others who really love and care for you. But you get so tied up in your own life and your own stuff that it's easy to forget those others until it's too late.

Yeah, that's great, Ty, but by the way, I have a real job and life sucks and

I'm glad you're able to travel around the world. (How my life is often seen by the other half.)

Even the cameraman I travel around with has the same issues. It appears he's having the time of his life traveling everywhere, but the truth is that he misses his family and he's kinda miserable at times. His job is to make sure everybody else is having a good time. But guys like us end up in this business because we realize what it takes. What I respect is someone who basically has my schedule but can also balance having a wife and children.

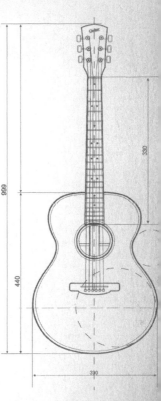

I've sent off for a catalog and a manual to figure this out. Because I do know the feeling of love. There's nothing better.

Love is realizing you're not walking to meet someone but you're running. And when you ask yourself why, you realize you're running to get back to this person you can't wait to be with. That's when you know it's something that will leave you out of breath. Those are the magical moments. But then sometimes you get back home and discover that family's dream has been started without you. So love turns to pain; things get weird; and then you start to turn callous and jaded and worn down. But you realize at some point that someone's gotta take care of you, right?

This is getting tiresome.

Let's just file Ty Pennington's Love and Relationships under the Success and Failure categories.

No. File them under Works in Progress.

8. "LOVE AIN'T FOR KEEPING" BY THE WHO.

"So, Ty. How's your love life?"

"Well, my love life is great. In my opinion love is where the laughter is. We all need more in our lives."

"So, Ty. Do you shed tears as much in your personal life as you do on the show?"

"No. And in fact, there are so many things I should have cried over but never did."

(9.) "I WANT TO KNOW WHAT LOVE IS" BY FOREIGNER. Telling someone how much I love them gives me the same sort of feeling I get when I see a sign that reads, "Live Love Laugh." A feeling like I'm going to puke. Love is something that should be seen and not heard—and signs that read "Live Love Laugh" shouldn't exist. To me, the moment you suddenly utter some Hallmark lines is the moment when trueness gets tossed out the window. I'm a firm believer that it's what you do that really matters. It's not enough to tell a family they'll get back on their feet; you need to go build them a house so they can, or show them how.

That being said, I know I'll eventually disappoint someone. Recently on *Trading Spaces* (the reboot), Paige told me she didn't want the woman we were designing a room for to be disappointed.

"I'm pretty sure I've disappointed every woman I've ever come across," I tell Paige. "So what's another bad room in the grand scheme of things?"

To say I'm complicated is an understatement.

"UNSATISFIED"

The true spirit and soul of an artist can be difficult to live with. If I frustrate myself, how much more irritating can life with an artist be for someone else?

Let me explain this inner frustration. It's a good/bad thing.

One of my favorite songs is "Unsatisfied" from one of my favorite bands, The Replacements. It sums up the artist in me: "Look me in the eye. Then tell me that I'm satisfied. Hey, are you satisfied?"

I think never being satisfied is the blessing and the curse of being creative. I think all of us want to prove to the world that we have something to offer, that we're special and have a talent. When I was younger, that's all I ever wanted. Someone to recognize my gifts, whatever they might be.

When I was in art school, I was a thrift store junkie. I'd go and buy jackets for a dollar and then throw paint on them and make them SUPER loud. I remember once making a jacket for my brother that had safety pins all over the lapel—this very punk jacket—and I thought it was basically garbage. Wynn, however, loved it. "That's one of the coolest jackets I've ever seen!" he told me. It had six different colors splashed over it. I'd wear a jacket like that and go out, strutting around like some kind of peacock, begging others to notice me. So I always wanted attention.

Finally after *Trading Spaces* and *Extreme*, I've gotten more than enough attention. I'd love to be able to say I'm completely content with everything I've ever done. I should be. Hey, I've helped build more than 220 homes across America with amazing builders and volunteers that changed the way people look at each other and their community. I've constructed eight structures and hospitals in impoverished Africa and have done TV shows in the UK. But at the same time, there's still a list of things I want to do. Strangely, getting married and having children aren't on that list. It's creative projects that I still never get around to doing.

For example, one big goal in the last few years has been to finish some art pieces created from incredible photos I've taken on trips around the world. I want to blow them up and then turn them into paintings. For three years, I've talked about doing this for an art show that happens annually. (Insert curse word right here.) Every year I try to do it, but another project shows up and something else distracts me. *Like writing a book.* So like a failed New Year's resolution, I tell myself I'm going to send the photos to someone, but I have them in a file and I never get around to loading them in a zip drive. (Insert another curse word right here.)

I get frustrated because I know what I'm missing. It's starting a creative project, knowing it will be fun painting new pieces. There's an elation in working on a project like this, so I get angry at myself, knowing I haven't even started the process. But I'll finish a job and come back home and then see the environment I'm surrounded by. All these boxes and clutter that need to be organized. A house that needs to be torn down and a new one that needs to be built.

Hello, chaos, my old friend. I've come to step over you again.

I'm not a stressed guy, but I stress myself out. I hate talking about how I'm going to do this or that project, but then these other jobs and shows lock down my time and my brain space. Art is a personal passion, just like music, so of course, deadlines take precedence. What has to be decided first? What's the most crucial problem at hand? For this art project, there's no deadline except one I put on myself. I'm all about making the deadline. A house in seven days. Or a book. Or a room.

Sometimes I look at other people who glide through life and don't put pressure on themselves. Man, I'd love to know how that feels. The pressure I feel is the pressure I put on myself to really take advantage of not only the talent I've been given but also the opportunities I have. I have friends who don't have the lucky life I have, and they'll tell me I should appreciate everything I have. And I do! But I also know I have only one go-round, so I feel I have to do everything I possibly can.

Not everybody can have opportunities to go on trips to exotic places where you can get these REAL photographs of REAL creatures in their environments. Like a hippo rolling around underwater and a crocodile sleeping with one eye open and a giraffe gliding across an African savanna. These are REAL moments I capture on film. I long to turn them into something to remember the moments, to get joy out of creating something with them, and then to hopefully make others feel the same way when they see them.

Pressure and frustration can be good things for an artist, because they challenge them to be as good as they can be and to do something new that will make them feel proud. Something that will fulfill them.

Another problem I encounter is the way I do art. I'm a designer, so sometimes I have to plan out a piece before I start working on it, and that's often anti-productive. The beauty of art is to dive into it without knowing the outcome. What paralyzes me mentally and what I can't stand about myself is that I'll dive into EVERYTHING. I'm the guy who went to Japan without knowing what would happen. So then why can't I do that on a canvas? Again, I overthink it.

Dude, just pick up a brush and do it! Sorry, just venting here.

Maybe there's some genuine fear involved. It's a gift to reach the pinnacle of success and do something that has incredible meaning for others on a show like *Extreme*. What sucks now is that anytime I do something new, I have to measure it against those things. I guess part of me is afraid that it's going to suck. But that's just part of life, right?

Yeah, your first painting's probably going to suck, but your second's going to be a little better, and your third will be an even better version of both of them.

I realize I can be as hard on others as I am on myself, without even meaning to be. It's like when I'd be on *Extreme* and initially someone comes up with this great idea. The team starts working while I'm flying off to the other show that's being taped. Then when I come back and see what they've done, I'll apply the Ty Pennington version of encouragement to my praise.

"You know what? That *actually* looks pretty good."

The problem is the italicized word *actually*. I say this as if I'm prepared to be disappointed. I realize I'm doing this one day and want to hit myself. I know I need to stop doing that. But this would constantly happen. Like the monkeys hanging off the ceiling. Even though they were hanging upside down, they looked pretty amazing. What happens is I come back just as tired as these helpers are, and yes, the room probably doesn't look as good as I want it to be. But I need to extend them some grace.

Okay, fine. It's only 80 percent close enough to what I wanted, but I should be happy with that ... I mean, I'm sure the Romans were happy when the aqueduct didn't work exactly right.

Setbacks *always* happen with every project. I'd see people being berated by other designers. "That's not what I wanted!" I'd see them leave in tears. I wonder what it'd be like if that's what your childhood looked like, to constantly be criticized. That's the very opposite of what nurtures good ideas. So I've learned to approach this in a positive way.

"It's nothing like what we discussed, but it's fantastic!" I'll say.

On *Extreme*, we don't have any time to change it anyway, so why berate someone? To be honest, they're the ones making the executive decisions, so who's to say their ideas are better than mine? I learn that if you want to create something amazing, you have to praise the people working for you, because they'll work twice as hard the next time. If you criticized them, then they won't care and won't try hard.

I think people have liked working with me. What I need to do is have this same attitude with myself, knowing that my creative endeavors won't always match the vision in my mind. Sometimes they turn out very differently, and sometimes that's a great thing.

The problem with finding time for art projects like this is that I'm always working on something. I have a buddy who once worked with me say that the only time he's ever seen me content is when I'm in the middle of another project. This is pretty accurate. I don't like the end, the finish line. I love the brainstorming and the eureka moments that happen. I love how wonderful they feel because they haven't been thought through yet, so there's unlimited potential and possibility for them.

> I love the brainstorming and the eureka moments that happen. I love how wonderful they feel because they haven't been thought through yet, so there's unlimited potential and possibility for them.

I guess it's in the moment of the creation that I'm perhaps the happiest. What brings me down is when I have to go out and repeat it over and over again, when I have to make sure it's exactly like it is the first time, when someone says something like, "We really like what you did last time, but can you do it in blue?" It's in the middle of the chaos, when the raw creation is coming together, when I don't know what it's going to look like in the end but knowing I'm heading in the right direction. That's my most joyous moments in the creative process.

I also guess—since I'm guessing a lot—that creative people sometimes have struggles in life because not everyone finds elation that's quite like this. People might work their butts off in service-oriented jobs that don't fulfill them the way art can. In the creative industry, we're so lucky that we have jobs where we come up with an idea and hope the idea is great and then hopefully have a great team to help execute it. That's the luckiest job you could ever have, and honestly, not everybody gets that lucky in life.

I get really sort of depressed when I'm not doing something. I'm actually starting to feel a little blue just talking about all these unfulfilled projects. I need to go paint something. Or maybe write a song. I'll be back in just a minute . . .

"GIMME SHELTER"

You're living the dream, and this is what the dream looks like.

Extreme Makeover: Home Edition is a bonafide success, and it's changing lives and connecting communities and exploding with incredible ratings. But you can't help but think of something Tom Forman, one of the show's executive producers, likes to jokingly say: "*Extreme Makeover: Home Edition*—changing lives across America while destroying our own."

He's partially right because you're on the road every day and your family is wondering where you are and when you're ever coming back home again. *Extreme* is such a huge outfit and takes so many people to get everything done, and that's just for one episode. But since you're Ty Pennington, you get the honor of doing two shows at once while simultaneously having absolutely no life.

This is your schedule: You show up with the cast and crew and surprise the family and get to know their story. Then you start the demolition on their house the second day. Right after that, you fly to another town to start work on an entirely different house with another family and a different cast and crew. You surprise the family and then do demo on the second day; then you fly back that night to finish your room for the big reveal the next day. After an exciting day of shooting the reveal and celebrating with everybody, you fly back to the other home, completely bushed and half the man you were at the start of the week. You finish another room and then have another reveal and another celebration. Then you get to go home and have three days to get everything else happening in your life finished, along with connecting with your loved ones and friends.

Yes, you're exhausted, but you have a home line of products that you've just started with Sears, so you need to figure out patterns for plates and glasses. And yes, you could just simply tell Sears to go ahead and design them and put your name on it, but you're not that kind of person. You know it's better and more Ty when you put your unique twist and special touch on it. So you refuse to delegate, and maybe you become a bit of a control freak with everything, but what are you going to do? What's the one thing you've always wanted as an artist? Recognition and success.

Exhaustion? Come on. You're designing rooms on TV and creating a product line that people are literally going to be putting on their beds and dinner tables. There's no way you're *not* going to do this. This is the life you've dreamed about, and now it's here. You are living the dream.

Of course, the problem with a dream is that it can turn into a nightmare because it's everything you wanted but it's all happening at once. And anybody who's had it will tell you to be careful about having too much of it, especially all at the same time.

The good thing is you're old enough not to be foolish enough to stand up on a table, shaking a bottle of champagne and screaming, "Let's party." You're not that dumb. (Well, maybe just one more bottle . . .) You're not going to go out and spend all the money. You're not going to go all MC Hammer and hire a staff of two hundred people, along with buying a helicopter and a bunch of horses with gold saddles and matching chaps.

You've experienced enough in your life not to look at money as if it's money. You don't trust money, nor do you believe you're always going to be this comfortable.

You know life is a roller coaster, and you know you never know what's going to come your way.

So in the midst of living the dream, the person suffering the most is the one you're trying to have a relationship with. If they're lucky, they get an eighteenth of your time, and they become stressed because they see you're stressed. You come back to town and they're excited and energetic and want to go out and celebrate and party and all you want is to sleep and get the hundred other things you need to do finished. But of course you love this person and want and need to be with them, so you become even more exhausted, trying to live life with them in the limited amount of time you have before heading back out to build two more houses and change a bunch more lives.

"FAKE PLASTIC TREES"

"Love is like a precious plant. You can't just accept it and leave it in the cupboard, or just think it's gonna get on with itself. You gotta keep watering it. You've got to really look after it, and be careful of it, and keep the flies off and see that it's alright, and nurture it."*

John Lennon sure was right when he said this. For me and my life, that water is either a downpour turning into a deluge, or it's just a drought waiting to be watered. And by the way, the water raining over my plant comes from tears.

Relationships, roots, families, friendships—they all require one thing. Georgia O'Keeffe sums it up best: "Nobody sees a flower—really—it is so small—we haven't time—and to see takes time, like to have a friend takes time."† That's true. And if friends require time, then what does someone we love need?

Marriage and commitment? Yeah, I was in a relationship for more

---

* "John Lennon 'Man of the Decade' Interview," 12/2/1969, transcribed by www .beatlesinterviews.org from video copy of archived interview.

† Quoted in Elizabeth Hutton Turner, *Georgia O'Keeffe: The Poetry of Things* (New Haven, CT: Yale University Press, 1999), 47.

than a decade. I've been *really* close. I've felt love firsthand, and I've also felt the ache of when it doesn't work out. The experience has made me realize things about myself.

I'm so used to the chaos of traveling in my life. It's comfortable to me. But I often wonder what else survives back home. Will a plant survive? No. A dog won't either. A cat might, but it will be an angry cat. So how can I keep moving and keep going and ever create any sort of stable life and family for myself?

Then I ask myself, *What's the goal, Ty? Am I going to be that constant stream in motion, forever hitting those rocks and going around them? Will I ever reach that river?* (Wow, this is getting deep. I'm so glad I'm sharing all my issues with you. Man, I love . . . love.)

My goal is to be constantly moving but staying in one place where I can be there for a person and a family and a dog and a plant and maybe even a whole garden. All while still feeling content with enough creative projects that keep me interested.

Maybe I should date myself. Then I'd realize how much I'm not around.

> *Maybe I should date myself. Then I'd realize how much I'm not around.*

It's funny. For a guy who's known for building homes and bringing families together and boosting love in others, I'm actually like a plant in the wind looking out a plane window. I feel this way sometimes. Like I'm a growing plant that's being shipped all over the country and looking for the right sunny spot where I can actually grow. But always, just as I start to get acclimated, I'm put back in a package and sent to another location.

I'm like a plant on a television show. "Yeah, we need that plant we used in scene 29a . . ."

I'm not only the person who makes people feel comfortable on a set, but I've become the plant that looks natural in whatever environment I'm constantly put in.

The truth is, at some point that plant (which is me) has to find a way to be in a location where all these needs are met. Yes, a plant needs to be watered, but doesn't it also need to stay in one place so it can develop roots?

I guess it's all how you look at it. Both the love and the pain. Sometimes they can become blurred, however. They can get frayed and numb. Like when you're trying to find the strength to forge on and forgive when a good friend somehow has a baby with the one you love. Trying to compartmentalize the anger, the confusion, the road to reason can be tricky things.

A simple house plant won't tell you what life's been like or what it's been through. It just finds a way to keep from wilting. Some days it looks weathered and sad; other days it looks like it just got back from someplace tropical, almost smiling with its palms. The plant has lived a real life, and it doesn't hide its scars. It just does its best to feel happy and to make you feel like you belong where you are. It doesn't have many talents, but the ones it has are designed to enhance your mood and make you feel . . . well, comfortable. And that in turn makes a simple plant happy.

Sometimes when a plant finally shuts up, it becomes a great listener . . .

My goodness. I need to write a children's book about a guy named Fern. *The Fate of Fern*.

"HIGH HOPES"

The minute I find out the Nick family's backstory on season 3 of *Extreme*, I know this is going to be a rough one emotionally. It's such a sad story, yet at the same time, it's one about believing in possibilities, believing you can make a difference. Imagining you will, and never ever giving up on hope. We learn this from Colleen Nick, whose favorite three words are *LOVE ALWAYS HOPES*.

The toughest part of this story is the not knowing. But there aren't many people around Alma, Arkansas, who don't know about Colleen Nick and her six-year-old daughter, Morgan. Listening to what Colleen tells the design team and me on their video as we ride toward Alma on the bus breaks our hearts. She describes the details of what happened one night ten years ago at a Little League baseball game, only a hundred yards from a police station in a small town where everybody knows almost everybody. Her account sends chills up our spines.

It's amazing how she remembers everything about that night. As a single mom raising three children, Colleen is spending the evening with Morgan as mother and daughter. They drive about fifty miles away from their house to Alma to visit friends and watch the game. It's a chance to spend time together.

Colleen's eyes light up as she talks about her six-year-old daughter sitting next to her in the bleachers. She recalls Morgan being very playful and sweet as she bends down and secretly unties Colleen's shoes. She even remembers Morgan's outfit.

As it starts to get dark and the game is in its final innings, other young kids ask Morgan to play with them and catch fireflies. At first Colleen says no, but Morgan continues to plead with her. Colleen remembers something she heard about not being overprotective as a parent, about letting children have more freedom to grow as individuals. So against her better judgment, she lets Morgan go catch fireflies but tells her to stay close, where she can see her.

Just moments later, with the game over and everyone heading to the parking lot, Colleen finds the other kids but can't spot her daughter. The other kids tell her Morgan was by the car dumping sand out of her shoes, but Colleen can't find her anywhere. In the car or on the field. The park is soon empty, and it's apparent that Morgan has vanished. The police are called, but the only clue to her whereabouts is a strange man in a red truck.

Morgan Nick is last seen at the age of six.

Police believe she's been abducted, but no one knows exactly what happened. Morgan has been missing for ten years. In fact, the day we pull up to Colleen's house and knock on the door is ten years to the day she was abducted. The search still continues, and Colleen has never given up hope that her daughter Morgan will one day come home. In fact, Colleen has turned her pain into something positive—the Morgan Nick Foundation, a nonprofit that searches for missing children, educates parents about safety, and has helped pass laws to make finding missing children easier.

Not a day goes by that Colleen doesn't think about Morgan and where she is or what happened. The nightmare plays over and over in her head. I can't even imagine the pain and torture it must be to not know. The Morgan Nick Foundation has helped to successfully find numerous missing children and bring them back home to their families. It's the hope that one more child might be found that keeps Colleen going.

Colleen has done all this while still raising her two other children, Logan and Taryn. They're young when Morgan vanishes, but they still miss their sister. Having someone in your family abducted and never knowing exactly what happened can leave a horrible dark cloud over everything. Happy days are seldom, and family reunions are usually days to remember Morgan.

Every June 9, the day she was abducted, the family gets together to remember and honor Morgan. Friends, neighbors, and townspeople gather with them at the high school near the field where Morgan was taken. They blow up pink balloons (Morgan's favorite color) and attach a photo of Morgan (what she'd look like now), along with a telephone number to call if anyone has seen her. "It's not a message in a bottle," Colleen says. "It's a message of hope."

We arrive a decade later on June 9, and instead of sending Colleen and her two children on vacation like we typically do after we surprise the family, I go with them to the local high school football stadium for their annual tradition. The thousands gathered there rise to their feet and cheer Colleen and her children as they enter. As she goes to the podium to thank everyone, just as she does every year, I look out at this assembled crowd and realize something.

These people don't consider Morgan's disappearance an issue just for the

Nick family. This entire community lost a child. It is their loss, shared among all these faces. Young, old, and some who probably didn't even live in the town when Morgan was taken. This gathering is remarkable since it's a way to keep hope alive. This *ceremony*, for lack of a better word, is the community's way of keeping Morgan's story out there. Just in case.

A saturated amber light fills the stadium as the sun starts to set behind us, and through that light comes the rest of Colleen's family, carrying 3,500 pink balloons. One for every day since Morgan's abduction. Through tears of sadness for Morgan and tears of joy at the poetic beauty of the moment, I join the community of Alma in silent prayer as those balloons begin to float above us, carrying that "message of hope."

I don't think you can put a gauge on loss. Is losing a child to illness worse than losing a child in a car accident? And how does that compare to having your happy, healthy daughter taken from you? I hope I never know. But what I do know is that I've seen what happens when a community embraces a family whose loss is beyond comprehension. I've seen the comfort it brings and the hope it generates. And I've seen the love. More than that, I've felt the love—and it's strong. I walk into that football stadium feeling like an outsider, yet I leave knowing that I will think of Morgan every June 9.

As the balloons for Morgan go higher in the sky, I grab my camera. Later, while looking at the shots, my eye is drawn to a single balloon that seems to be heading off on a different path. Is it naive to hope that maybe this is the balloon whose card will fall to the ground and be picked up by someone who has some information to help the Nick family?

Our goal this week is like the goal we have every week on *Extreme*—to give back a little joy and happiness to a family who absolutely deserves and needs it. The time with the Nick family and the people of Alma is a reminder of the bond and connection you can have with a community. It's what makes people feel they belong. It's not always where you're raised, but where you want to put down roots. A place where you can grow, watch your children grow, and feel you're part of something bigger than just your street or your yard.

There's no way we can do our show and our jobs without the help of the communities, neighbors, families, and friends. After a while on *Extreme*, people start to follow us to another state and volunteer again! Instead of Grateful Dead fans, now it's grateful people! I literally call them our homies. This is our show's legacy—the impact we have on communities and other people. It's neighbors working together and getting to know each other. Having fun.

I don't know the true meaning of the word *community* before I start *Extreme Makeover: Home Edition*. For me, the connection and bond I've had with communities all over America is overwhelming. It really gives me hope in humanity to see people from every walk of life come to lend a hand, give a cheer of support, cook a meal, give a hug, pick up a hammer, and then welcome a family home!

I love my job on *Extreme*.

I love the country we travel throughout.

I love what can be done when we work together.

Day

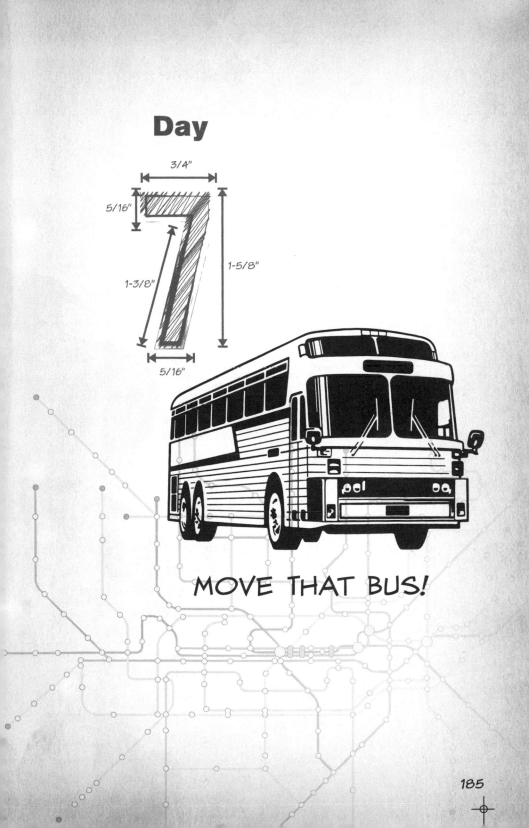

7

3/4"

5/16"

1-5/8"

1-3/8"

5/16"

MOVE THAT BUS!

Move That Bus!

"SEVEN SEAS OF RHYE"

kay. We've reached the final day. Prepare to be moved. To cry tears of joy. To laugh out loud. To want to start at the beginning again, now that you realize the amazing twist of the story. What's the twist? I don't know—I still have one more chapter left to figure it out.

The seventh and final day on *Extreme* is not a day of rest, but it is a day of celebration. You've reached the end. The payoff is here. The journey is coming to an end, and you're going to leave feeling a little better about yourself and life.

That's how I'm feeling about writing this last chapter too. I'm hoping to leave you feeling warm and cozy. Maybe you'll even give me a big hug. Well, not me literally, but you can give the book a nice squeeze. I'm sure it's going to have my face on it somewhere.

Maybe you can even give it a nice kiss. Kinda like the one a woman gives me after she is so moved at the bedroom I design for her. I give her this gift she could never give herself, so she just loses it and gives me this massive hug and kiss that is really long and awkward. But I understand. She is truly overjoyed.

So keep reading. And it's perfectly fine if you want to kiss me when you're finished.

"UNDER PRESSURE"

Knowing a family is supposed to walk into their new house in front of thousands of their neighbors and friends is a good enough deadline to keep you motivated. Deadlines are the key to finishing anything. But so is not overthinking.

I love it when I hear an art teacher or someone else say, "We want you to THINK BIG." As if size matters. In short, SIZE does matter, but sometimes thinking big is just overcompensating. Actually, it's overthinking that's the problem.

One of my favorite magazine ads from the late '60s was for the VW Beetle. The caption under a photo of the car was "Think Small." It was so simple. Two words said so much, especially with the price of gas skyrocketing. The campaign won awards for its to-the-point simplicity.

I think there's a bigger message to thinking small. In my case, I tend to overthink everything, especially when it comes to my art and design and even my music. Sometimes we all put so much pressure on ourselves to overachieve (cue David Bowie and Freddie Mercury singing "Under Pressure"). It's crazy how many obstacles we can create for ourselves while we're trying to prove to the world we have talent.

Here's a great example. I've basically been drawing and painting things since I was five years old. I've designed and built hundreds of functioning sculptures. But in all this time, I've really only had maybe two art shows, and I think one was a mockumentary about an artist who collects garbage . . . Yes, *Adis Pozal* again.

The only other time I actually showed my work was when someone signed me up for a large group show and there was a clear deadline and date where lots of eyes would see my work. I cranked out a lot of pieces that were black ink illustrations and were cool. I just didn't think they were good enough. So I created four new pieces combining painting, illustration, graphic-designed tattoo-like images, and textural patterns—all put together like building blocks or puzzle pieces a child might put together to explain what's happening in his life. A self-portrait in different images. But even this didn't seem good enough.

This type of BIG THINKING still goes on today. Remember the art show I mentioned in the last chapter? I seriously mark it on my calendar every year. The only problem is the project keeps getting pushed to the back burner. It's really just a matter of trying to put it together between jobs. (And if you're wondering why I'm mentioning it for the second time, I'm wanting to put these words in print so someone holds me accountable to finally getting it done!)

Let's face it, work always comes first, and we are all happy to be working. But even as I write this, I'm working on designing a basement man cave for a guy who is a huge Georgia Bulldogs fan for a show called *While You Were Out* on HGTV and TLC. So there's the crazy chaos and pressure of not only finishing this book but also finishing this room before he comes back home!

Here's the thing, I've been putting all this pressure on myself to create these amazing paintings for an art show *that may never actually happen*. Ha. But that's when I get a pretty cool idea. Since we're pretty much designing a men's lounge in this guy's basement, complete with dark-stained oak panels that Hildi wanted to put over the walls covered in gray flannel. Why not make it look like a gallery room, complete with portraits of different bulldogs that have a historic feel, as if they were all members of an elite Dog House membership?

With only fourteen hours before the big reveal, I start painting these vintage picture frames flat black that I found at a nearby thrift store. Since each frame has a different style and size, I decide to make the art look like it's done by different artists.

So here I am, painting and drawing all these different portraits of bulldogs. Layering some with watercolors, some with oil paints, and some with white chalk on black background. As I hang each of these custom art pieces in a newly designed gallery for a guy I haven't even met yet, I stop and realize what's happening.

Wow. I've just created my own art installation, and I'm having a show.

Instead of having to go to a gallery, the gallery will come to life through television.

The point to all this is that in one day and one late night, I create something I haven't been able to do for years. All because I have a DEADLINE. The room has to get finished, so this means the artwork has to be created. So instead of thinking BIG and making gigantic pieces that feel huge and bold, like I seem to always like, I decide to THINK SMALL and just do small picture frames that not only make the room work but make *me* work.

When my colleagues on the show see the art, they can't believe it.

"I knew you could design, but I had no idea you could draw and paint like that," Hildi says to me. "And I've known you for years."

Sometimes when you don't try to make a master-piece, you give yourself room to make mistakes. And mistakes are where the greatest ideas come from. In fact, I feel like it may have been a mistake to think I can actually finish writing a book in seven days, especially with all these other deadlines. But don't worry, I'm pretty sure this won't be a masterpiece. But I know it'll be what Mom used to say about me all the time: "a real piece of work."

Sometimes when you don't try to make a masterpiece, you give yourself room to make mistakes.

"WAITIN' FOR THE BUS"

It's funny to think that buses have played a big part in my life. There's the soiled underwear moment, and the moment I feel a warm, fuzzy feeling for the girl I'm standing next to. And there's the chaos I create while riding in the school bus, trying to convince my classmates to come to the football game.

"I'm gonna be watching *Gilligan's Island*," someone says.

"You can't do that! We have a football game to play behind the tennis courts!"

I sprint to the top of the bus and then run back, diving to see how many rows I can get past. Everybody hits me with their forearms, eventually getting so pumped up that they're all like, "We're coming!"

Then there's the bus on *Extreme*. The show gets a tour bus to save money by having us sleep on it instead of staying at hotels. It's also an air-conditioned place we can go between shots. This will be the bus where I show the video to the designers, and the same one that will eventually move so the family can see their new home.

Who knew that screaming, "Move that bus!" would become a favorite catchphrase for *Extreme*? When I think of these three words today, a lot of things come to mind. I think of the families we've impacted. The houses we've built. The places we've visited. The communities and neighborhoods we've touched. The crews making everything happen. Most of all, I think of the individuals who have built me up and touched my life.

"HARDER, BETTER, FASTER, STRONGER"

Extreme Makeover: Home Edition is truly an example of a perfect storm of everything that works for a television show. You need to have extreme elements, a crazy amount of people who want to do this, real and genuine people who are invested in it. And you always have to outdo what you did last year. This is exactly what happens. We go from simply building a house legitimately in seven days (*simply*, ha!) to building a house and a community center or a house and a BMX track. We constantly outdo ourselves, and I love it.

All the while, the focus remains on one particular family. People watch every episode, and let's face it, you know the outcome of the show *every single time.* You're not surprised when a new house is built! But you get hooked into the story. You can't help it.

Extreme is basically *Trading Spaces* on steroids—bigger, more explosive, more dynamic, and definitely more emotional. The timing is perfect. With cable TV and with the political landscape. Nowadays people are more interested in *Game of Thrones* and streaming an entire season of something on Netflix. Back then, our show simply works. I remember being horrified when *Extreme* beats out *Arrested Development* in its ratings. I mean, what? It's one of the funniest and greatest shows ever.

Having a phenomenon like *Extreme* means you've reached the top of the creative mountain. Once you're there, everything you do afterward will be compared to what you've already done. I'll realize this on my last season of the show.

This is what it's like to be in a rock band. To come out with an amazing album that defines an era. One that people say may be the best album of the last decade.

After that, all you're remembered by is that album. Unless you come out with another. Sure, the band will still go out and perform and might still write albums because that's what they enjoy doing, but they'll almost always be compared to that BIG one.

For *Extreme*, it's about the right concept and the right group of people coming together at the right time. On *Trading Spaces*, I'm a smart-aleck carpenter, but on *Extreme*, I'm both the jokester and the guy having all these deep conversations. One moment I'm Gonzo from *Sesame Street*, and the next I'm Barbara Walters.

Someone at a diner once came up to me and couldn't believe they were meeting me.

"You're Ty Pennington! You don't know this, but you changed my life. I went into interior design because of your show back in the day."

"Awesome," I say. "Glad to hear it."

"No, you don't understand. It gave me a career. I have a business now, all because of you."

"Glad things worked out for you. Would you mind passing the salt?"

It's honestly surreal, thinking I can make such an impact on someone. Especially me, that kid causing chaos . . . Yeah, it always seems to go back to the boy wearing parts of his school desk, causing mayhem!

"NO SLEEP TILL BROOKLYN"

Here's a cool fact. In all those years on *Extreme*—nine seasons, 220-something houses—I never missed a day of work. Even if I was sick, I worked through it. I think this shows how important a belief in something positive really is—a belief in yourself that you are an *energy*, a beacon for others to follow.

I think this shows how important a belief in something positive really is—a belief in yourself that you are an energy, a beacon for others to follow.

If you act tired, your team will act tired. If you don't show up, your team won't give 100 percent. A leader leads; they don't complain. (Well, maybe in private. Ha!) But they don't focus on the negatives. (*These are horrible conditions. Too many long hours. Blah blah blah.*) A leader finds a way to make people believe in them because for that moment they will believe in themselves.

I'm proud of a lot of things in my life, but one of those is the fact that I never took a day off from *Extreme*. The only time I had to have someone fill in for me was when we decided to do four additional Hurricane Katrina relief shows while we were still working on two other shows. That's six shows going at the same time. It's safe to say that the team knew I was spent. I couldn't remember or even say the names of the designers on the bus because my body and brain had maxed out. No more bandwidth.

So who did they bring in? Mr. Kermit the Frog himself. That's right. I had a frog stand in for me while I recovered. Amazing.

Kermit, well, isn't really even human, but to this day he's my favorite celebrity I've met because he signed his headshot for me: "Thanks, Ty, for letting me host your show for you . . . it was the best time I ever had." Seriously, what kind of frog is that nice and well-mannered? Kermit. It's not easy being green.

Okay, Marlee Matlin also filled in on the episode when we helped out the Oregon School for the Deaf. But my point is, when you really believe in something, that something isn't the same without you. You become what that something is. And Kermit felt that love . . . that energy. He knew I had the best job in the world. Because whether it's a job or a calling, when you help change a person's life for the better, you change your own in the process.

Whether it's a job or a calling, when you help change a person's life for the better, you change your own in the process.

In the words of Forrest Gump, "And that's all I have to say about that."

"DO YOU REALIZE??"

Day Seven on *Extreme* is always about joy and gratitude. It's really such a beautiful experience, time after time after time. On *Trading Spaces*, I compete against myself to do a better room than I did last time, but the goal on *Extreme* is different. It's always to do the best design that will have the most amazing effect on someone's life.

It's funny, this journey I've gone on in design. I wrote a book about how good design can change lives, and it can. The thing is, as an artist, the greatest reward and satisfaction and gratification for something I've designed is to see the effect it has on the person or the group I'm doing it for. In my younger years, it was always about me showing off my talent to see if I could get a reaction. What's so great about *Extreme* is there's finally a different reason to show off your talents. You get to show how big of an effect it can have on someone else's life.

When you focus on something that's really important to somebody else, you will see the spirits of people lifted up and their lives changed. Talk about feeling joy and gratitude. Like our last two shows—perhaps our best ones—when we build seven homes in seven days for victims of the tornado that hit Joplin, Missouri. This is when the show is doing something good not just for ratings but to help as many people as possible. We even have Amish people showing up, not wanting to be on camera but simply wanting to help. *That's* what it should be all about!

As I reminisce about days of old (wow, that makes *me* sound old), I can't help being filled with gratitude. When I start to think about all these things that have been built, all these homes that have been created, it sorta blows my mind. I look back on *Trading Spaces* and think about the cabinet I built for Hildi made out of bamboo and painted canary yellow, or a bed made out of Brazilian mahogany that I slaved over and left in a home I'll never see again, knowing they're two of the nicest pieces I've ever made.

The joy comes in knowing I've put my touch on them. That I've handcrafted this one-of-a-kind item for someone. I don't even know what the value would be. I'm sure I appreciate it more than anybody else, because I know how unique it is to make. I also know I'll never do that design again. It's a one-time deal. You leave it and move on to the next. But at that moment, it's the greatest thing you've ever made and completed. The thing you're the proudest of.

Then with *Extreme*, you add that human connection. Whatever you're creating has to be amazing because these people need this, because they've been through so much and they need a new chapter written for their lives.

The rewarding part is knowing you gave them your best. That's it. That's the success. The failure is only giving half your effort. I can never fail in that way. I always have to make sure that whatever I'm doing is the best it can possibly be with whatever materials I'm working with—even in the recent episode of *Trading Spaces* I did where they tried to make me quit putting up wallpaper because it's a nightmare.

"We have to get outta here, Ty. We have to stop so we can finish before midnight."

"Well, get your shot and then go take lunch. In the meantime, I'll finish the ceiling. We're not going to say on camera, 'You know what? I'm quitting. You're right. It's just too much. I can't do it.' Well, no, that's not who I am."

Then I break the fourth wall and look into the camera. "Quitters is for rehab," I yell. "Why strive for excellence when you can just be average? I don't worship the Greek god named Mediocrates!"

Despite having some fun with that scene, it's true. I'm always—*always*—striving to give a design or a piece of furniture or a room

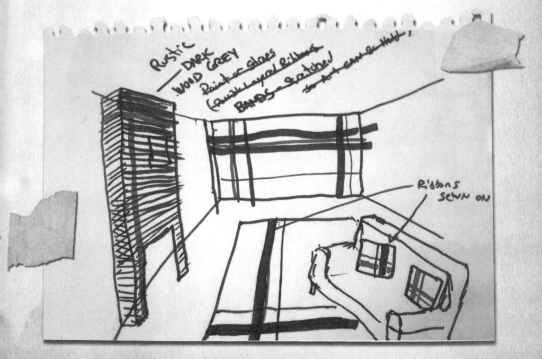

everything I can. I'm grateful to say that some of the best pieces of art I've ever produced have been for *Extreme*. They're rooms that have really gone above and beyond any sketch or drawing I can ever do, because not only are they functional, but they're having a lasting impact—not on *me*, but on *somebody else*.

That's what it's all about after spending a lifetime doing art. It's about finally having the opportunity to do something that really changes the life of somebody else. You realize this is as good as it gets when you're doing anything creative in art. When it really has a bigger effect than just whether you think it looks cool on a wall.

Then let me add this. I'm doing this surrounded by a group of people I dearly love. I'll be honest. I've said good-bye to many people in my life, but when *Extreme* ends, all of us on the show realize this particular chapter of our lives is ending. It's the saddest thing I've ever had to do just to say good-bye to the crew of people I've worked with for almost a decade.

I grew up in a family full of sarcasm where we don't take anything seriously. My brother would watch *Extreme* and say, "You want me to believe this sappy stuff?" I'd always be like, "Dude, it's real."

I've never experienced something like the community on *Extreme* simply because I never had that. You're dealing with real issues, and you're also connecting in a deeper way with the people you're in the trenches with.

Design can change *your* life (I've said that before, right?)—not just the lives of the people whose environment you're changing. *My* life changes because I'm part of a bigger family and a bigger team going around the country doing great things. We're really doing miracles.

It's powerful to see human beings decide to put their lives on hold and do something for others. You not only get to see gratitude, but you feel it as well. You get more. Two turns into four turns into eight and then turns into sixteen. That force grows, and since human beings can do great things together, any obstacles will just get out of the way.

I'm grateful, and I can't help but ask myself at times those two little words: *What if?*

"WHAT IF"

Funny how life evolves, how each action causes a reaction. Each door that closes creates another door that opens. This makes me think of common signs on doors and how it would be nice if life contained those as well: "Caution! Open Door Slowly!" "Do Not Open Door, Alarm Will Sound." "Please Use Other Door." "Caution! Toxic Gas."

But instead of warnings and explanations, we simply enter a new space wondering what might happen next. I think all those opening and closing doors in life should have signs that read, "WHAT IF?"

WHAT IF I hadn't surprised my mother that day in elementary school? Or seen the sad look of disappointment when she knew I was uncontrollable? What if I had not been creating chaos or wearing my desk, instead just sitting there calm and collected? Well, I'm pretty sure she would've never known how bad I really was, or that I had a real learning disability.

In fact, it's possible I could've gone on creating so much havoc for years that eventually I'd just be sent to a juvenile detention center. Yeah. Seriously. If my mom hadn't been interested in child psychology, she could've just ignored it, and studies say that five out of ten people in prison have some form of ADD and were never diagnosed. Now how different would THAT have been. Yikes.

WHAT IF I never read those first aid manuals that one time and didn't know what to do when my mom broke her leg? Wait. Let's maybe not go here. Moving on . . .

WHAT IF I had never used my dad's matches to start what would become a raging forest fire that nearly demolished an entire neighborhood? Well, that would've been great because I wouldn't have been horribly punished. But you see? That's the point. I wouldn't have learned how one stupid mistake can destroy everything, including the trust you have with your family.

WHAT IF I had never gone to that modeling agency on that day and at that time and met that smiling Japanese guy with a plane ticket? I may have just stayed at my graphic design desk job until I was eventually fired for breaking the glass on the expensive copy machine while Xeroxing my naked butt cheeks. True story. Yeah. How do you explain *that* on your résumé? "What was your reason for leaving?" "Hmmmm. I sorta showed too much of myself." Anyway. I wasn't fired—just let go for a few days. And then I moved to New York. Sometimes you gotta leave your BEHIND in the PAST . . . Wow. My future could've been so different.

WHAT IF I'd had a strong family foundation and lived with a happily married couple like on *The Brady Bunch* on TV? How different that would've been. How happy, how perfect. But if I hadn't had any cracks in my foundation and hadn't heard how hard and loud unhappy marriages can be, not to mention wondering who and what my real father was, then I wouldn't have rebelled against authority and everything. And if I hadn't been a complete jackass as a teen, I wouldn't have been asked to leave the house and go live on my own at the age of seventeen.

If it weren't for those horrible circumstances, I would never have learned a real hands-on trade or learned how to provide for myself. Those harsh working conditions led me toward the art of constructing and building real structures with my hands, much like the three-story tree house that was built because I was being punished and once again banned from the house. It could have all turned out so different. Oh no. I just had this vision of me in my fifties, without ever learning a skill and still living with my mother. Wait—half of that is actually a reality.

WHAT IF I didn't flip out of the Jeep at 70 mph? Or left my portfolio of pictures in my brother's car? What if I'd never lost all that skin on my backside? Wow . . . who knows. I could've become the first model to be known for their derrière. I could've been bigger than J.Lo, Beyoncé, or even, yep, the Kardashians. My backside modeling could have taken me to new heights. My face wouldn't be that famous, but those cheeks would be on billboards everywhere. Wow. I would've been so proud. But seriously . . . If I hadn't wrecked the Jeep and my body or lost my book. Thank you, Wynn. The homeless guys loved my 8x10s.

If none of that happened, I could have stayed in that business forever, just scraping by (no pun intended) on whatever job came my way. But that wasn't my trajectory. No, mine was so much more painful. My destiny (child), if you will, was putting a solid end to that career so I would have to focus and go back to what I was always good at—working with my hands and, of course, occasionally showing just a bit of my backside. You're welcome.

"DON'T STOP BELIEVIN'"

I still remember waking up in the corner of a warehouse when a piece of the ceiling falls on my head right after a bus rumbles by outside and hits the sewer grate. I'm in the warehouse district of Atlanta in a building built in 1867, wiping the chunks of plaster off my face while I fall out of bed. I look at the bottle of Gatorade in the corner and notice it's full of urine from the previous few nights. One thought fills my mind: *life's going to get better than this*. (Then another thought tells me to fill a bottle.)

I'm thirty years old, and I realize that some people my age already own their own business while I'm squatting in a warehouse taking care of my business in a plastic bottle.

Life is full of peaks and valleys. This moment is one of the latter (and a full bottle).

At this point I'm not finding much success in life, but I'm still having fun with my brother and bandmates and friends. I feel as if I have more of a family and am more connected than ever before. And I've come to believe there are different levels of feeling like a success in life. And I haven't felt success too many times in my life. But it's also how you define that word.

Sure, *success* can mean standing with a team of people receiving an Emmy Award. Winning an award that says you did something in a competitive category in a tough industry. But true success is knowing you're on a show that's actually making people's lives better instead of running them over and exploiting them to make entertainment.

The moment you go on stage, all you can think about are the people you work with day in and day out. The award for "Outstanding Reality Show" really belongs to the people in the trenches who make all this happen, over and over again. Success isn't holding that award in my hand; it's having a show receive awards for doing something to make a difference.

No amount of satisfaction about *Extreme* will ever compare to the victory and the high of the final moments on the show when we bring the family home. Honestly, you feel like you're on top of the world when you look out a window toward the street in front of the new house. The bus waits there, along with the other designers. You take one last look at this room you're putting the final touches on.

This looks awesome. They're going to love it.

Then you run out the door and yell, "We've finished the house! Let's bring them home!"

The entire world explodes in cheering and pandemonium. You look around to see a line of people going for a mile in every direction, all waiting to welcome the family home. You run down the street high-fiving people you've never met. This is not only the greatest day of this family's life, but it's the greatest day of your life too. That's the sort of emotions you feel.

For a second, you turn around and go back to the house, remembering you have a job and you also have ADHD. Hoping you remember all the things you're supposed to say, get all the family names right, and make sure to thank the builders and all that good stuff.

Then you bring them out of the car, and you say, "Move that bus!" and then you actually visualize what change in a life looks like. For a moment you see hope designed right there in front of you.

I don't know if there is a higher pinnacle you can reach in a television show. Or really in life in general.

What you did with your mind and your hands creatively, along with the power of volunteering neighbors . . . People who want to do good things . . . Seeing what that looks like in the shape of a house . . .

Unbelievable.

For me, this is as good as it gets. It's why I build houses.

> *Look at what good people can do when they put their minds together to make someone's life better.*

No "success" in life is ever going to top this. No walk down the red carpet and no holding a trophy in my hand will ever compare to such a moment. How can I ever top this? Climbing Mount Everest isn't going to happen; I like oxygen way too much. This is our Mount Everest.

For the families, it's a feeling like the world cares about you. People want to celebrate you and want you to have the best day of your life.

All of us want to feel special, right? This comes out in different ways for everybody. For us artists, we have to create something. How cool is it to create a whole new chapter in someone else's life?

Sometimes in the middle of this, I'll remember that messed-up kid or angry teen or lost punk rocker living in the warehouse, and I'll wonder what I'm doing here.

And not only am I here, but I'm the ringmaster. I'm also the guy the family is telling their story to, the sympathetic guy who is shedding tears as he listens. Everywhere I'll go from here on out, I'll be known as the guy who makes people cry and who does the same while consoling them. I never cried as a teen, not even after getting kicked out of my house. But now, when a single mom is telling me her struggles or a son is talking about losing his parents or someone is opening up for the first time as they tell their story, why wouldn't you cry? How can you not?

I've gone from being the funny jokester-instigator-comedian-carpenter on *Trading Spaces* to being the guy who's having serious conversations about what people have gone through and reassuring them that things are going to be okay.

"Don't worry about it—we're going to take care of it for you. You go on vacation with your family, and in a week you're going to have a new house."

How'd I become that guy?

I don't know for sure, but I think people can see that I've been through some of my own rough spots in life. I think that's why I easily connect with these individuals, because we've all met and known someone who's lost someone and something.

I've become a combination of Santa Claus and Barbara Walters! (Which would look like a band member of the New York Dolls.) Not that I studied the art of doing good interviews. I just realize that sometimes you don't have to say anything. Sometimes you just let a person talk and share their story. And as soon as I see these strangers are actually believing in me, I start to do a better job.

I'm grateful the show allows me to see parts of myself I don't even know exist. Parts my brother *still* doesn't believe are true.

"Oh boy," Wynn tells me. "You got the whole world fooled! What? You're really this kindhearted guy they show?"

"Yeah. Maybe I am."

He still remembers that homeless guy knocking on his door to borrow his bathroom, or the teenager setting his shoes on fire. (True story.)

"Look, Wynn. Now I'm helping people with their problems."

"Oh yeah? Well I've got problems too! After you're done fixing everybody else's problems, can you come over and unclog my toilet?"

Success is always how you see it.

"BEAUTIFUL CHILD"

As an artist, I find it hard to know when a painting is actually finished. When is enough . . . enough? When is one more stroke overdoing it? I think sometimes the most beautiful things are the simplest and purest, left to be magical without too much overthinking. I also think we're all amazing pieces of art . . . We're all works in progress. Each of us starts out as a rough sketch, and then our lives become shaped with strokes, splatters, and imprints of color and personality. Just as we start to become recognized as a silhouette of some type of object, we start to see a resemblance. It's not exact, but it's obvious. The art has been influenced by another artist. It's been enhanced because it wants to emulate what inspired it.

When I look back at my life as a work in progress, I see now the things that changed my blank canvas. From the primer to the early sketches, it was hard to see the direction my painting was headed. Especially with all the spills, stains, scratches, and mistakes. They all create layered textures and patterns that haven't been exposed yet to other techniques, cultures, and experiences.

Over time, the painting starts to show signs of talent and originality because it's being exposed to new ideas and mediums. Then, most importantly, the creation is inspired by other artists who stand out because they have a passion and a cause we all want to be a part of. It's because of these incredibly strong and driven artists that we start to change.

We "works in progress" become deeper and richer, and we reflect emotion. We start to tell a story that matters—a story that makes a difference—because we are influenced by a story stronger than our own. One that's heavier, harder, and more painful than we know how to express. These are the influences that really impact and change you, that set you apart from what you were before you met them.

Sometimes that amazing influence can be a little eight-year-old girl fighting a reoccurring monster called cancer, a fight that's hard to win. That little girl's name is Boey, and she changes the way I look at life forever.

When I think about all the deserving families we help on *Extreme*, there's one family I always get choked up about, even when I'm just talking about them in interviews. It's not that the Byers family is so different from any other. In fact, it's just the opposite. They're a family that seems so familiar. Almost as if they live on your street maybe three doors down. They're the family at every community sporting event and backyard barbecue, the one laughing and shouting and having fun. It's like we all know them, like they're just like us, except for this one thing . . . their youngest daughter, Boey, is fighting cancer for the second time.

Cancer is a horrible disease that can kill a family's spirit, yet the Byers family's spirit is stronger than any I've ever seen. The backbone of that spirit is Boey. She's fought the monster of cancer once already and beat it, and in the process, she's realized how many kids going through chemotherapy don't even have a stuffed teddy bear to hold on to or to cry into when no one is looking. Having gone through chemo herself, she knows how horrible it can be, so she wants to make a difference.

So Boey raises money selling whatever it takes, finding a way to bring a stuffed, fluffy teddy bear to every kid in that hospital. Literally in her weakest moments, she finds the strength to think about others suffering the same fate. Who does that at the age of eight?

When I ask Boey what it was like finding out her cancer had come back, she can't find the words. Because there are no words to describe complete devastation. There are no words to describe what it's like to look into your parents' eyes and see their fear of knowing the inevitable. Having to be strong every single day when as parents you have to subject your daughter to more chemo and radiation even as she's saying out loud, "Please, I'd rather die than go through that again." How do you fully describe that? You can't.

The thing about meeting Boey is that she acts like an adult. So smart, educated, and well-spoken. It's like talking to an old soul in a young, battle-stricken body. It's hard to imagine what it's like to be a kid who never really gets to have a childhood. Think about it—she loses her hair because of the chemo, and then just as it starts growing back in, she gets the news that the cancer is back and she has to lose it all over again. I love that her father shaves his head to let her know they are going through this as a family. That alone crushes me. It reminds me of losing my cousin to leukemia in high school and seeing his classmates all shaving their heads in support.

I think we've all known someone or a family that's been affected by the horrors of cancer. It's awful—that's all you can say. Cancer just sucks. Maybe that's why we all feel so connected to this family. My desire is to give Boey a bit of the childhood that cancer has taken away, so I make her room my special project and design her very own little fashion boutique, complete with clothes, branding, and, of course, a closet full of shoes and colorful wigs—something an eight-year-old girl shouldn't have to wear, but if she has to, she may as well look super swank while doing so.

I'll always remember her face as she walks into her new room. It's the face of an angel feeling joy and happiness for the first time in a while.

A joy that's inspired by her spirit of strength and giving despite her circumstances of need. I only spend a moment in time with Boey, but that little human being with a gigantic spirit inside has a lasting impact on who I am today.

She affects so many people, including a very stern, rugged, dry-witted, and sarcastic oak of a man I'll refer to as Connelly. He's a friend and fellow coworker from Boston who's part of the circus (aka life on the road) of a never-ending television show. A show that not only builds houses in seven days but tells amazing and true stories of families that may just live next door. Connelly laughs, but he never cries. Ever. Until he meets Boey.

Boey and the Byers family impact so many lives. Boey's story inspires other kids, along with other families, to fight hard and give the gift of hope. To never quit believing in the power to overcome all obstacles. Boey gives something to this world. She gives us the meaning of strength, love, family, and hope. She inspires us all to never step away from a challenge. Even a challenge as big as finding a cure for cancer.

"I BELIEVE IN YOU"

Sometimes there are doors that open and people who walk through them who can literally change your life. One of those people is Nancy Neil, the woman who gave me my first job. Rob Marish, our cameraman, is another, a guy with a sick sense of humor who you want to work with as much as possible because he makes you laugh, and that's what you need, especially if you have a stressful television job.

Then there's Denise Cramsey from Allentown, Pennsylvania, a woman who not only affects every person she works with but ultimately will change who you are forever. She's a hardcore Pittsburgh Steelers fan from an Irish Catholic family. She's what I affectionately call a badass.

I first meet Denise when she's a producer on *Trading Spaces*. Like me, they offer her a $50 raise, and she ends up leaving. She's actually another reason for me to leave as well. *If you're going to treat her that way, well . . .*

After the first season of *Extreme*, as they consider the idea of building two houses at the same time, I go to the male producer and recommend he hires Denise.

"Look, I know you need an A-team and a B-team, and no offense, but you need to hire a female," I tell him. "We're talking about nurturing and caring for people. And the things you're telling me in my ear aren't that nurturing or caring. See if Denise is available."

Sure enough, Denise is hired, not because of me, but because she's great at her job. Her first week is truly memorable. I remember being astounded that she doesn't bail after her first episode is shot. Yeah, it's *that* bad.

Here's a good lesson about coming into a job you think you're prepared for. Everybody wants to be on a show like *Extreme*, one that's getting great ratings and people are talking about. But few ever expect to be handed that dream job and then have everything (and I mean *everything*) go wrong.

We're working outside in New Orleans, helping a woman who recently lost her husband and oldest son in a car crash. She's raising her three young sons in a farmhouse. It's been raining for days before we get there, so the soil turns into a thick, gray mud—a mud so thick that it stops the machines from working since gunk is getting caked onto the chains. Then to add to that, we start having issues with the builder. The first sign that something is wrong is when I go to him with a concern.

"Hey, I don't want to seem alarmed, but I don't see any Latinos working on this construction job. In my book that's a bit of a problem. That's a red flag. Those guys are on every site, and that's why it gets done."

The builder just gives me this attitude, saying he doesn't hire Latinos and telling me, "This is all American-made here." Soon it becomes a real nightmare as he demands more money to build the home. In the end, we have to bring in another builder, but by then, we're two days behind.

So when I see Denise, she's on the site, wearing these big sunglasses that make her look like a 1950s Catwoman. She's probably hiding her eyes since she's stressed, and she's probably been crying. The first day on the job, and she has to deal with a guy who shut down all construction. The morale is low; it's been raining nonstop; the talent doesn't know what to do.

We're in trouble, I begin to realize.

So when I show up on-site, only three workers are there, waiting on the others to come. Just at that moment when you think everything's about to fold, Denise comes out to talk to the entire team.

"Look, guys, I'm not going to sugarcoat it," she tells us. "We're in a bad spot. This could be the first *Extreme* that doesn't get done . . . But it's not going to be that way. Because it's not going to happen on my watch!"

Then she plays something on the bus speakers that she and Robin Samuels, the story producer, have set up. It's John Belushi's hilarious motivational speech from *Animal House*.

"What? Over? Did you say 'over'? Nothing is over until we decide it is! Was it over when the Germans bombed Pearl Harbor? Hell, no!"

Despite some much-needed levity, Denise is totally serious about rallying the troops.

"I don't know if any of you have experienced this before, but I'm letting you know, I'm not going to sleep! I'm not going to stop until we find a way to build this home for this family!"

Here's a nurturing woman who's been hit in the face with adversity, looking like she's going to fail miserably on her first show. But Denise doesn't back down. When another builder finally shows up, we have to push back the start of the house by a day. All I remember from that week is scraping all the caked-up mud off the porch. When the mom and her sons come back home, they have no idea of the struggles that went on during the week, nor should they. I see Denise proudly looking at the monitor and seeing the reveal—watching a brave woman looking at her brand-new house and new life.

Denise succeeds in her first show, despite having a contractor revolt and try to hijack the show. I know at that moment, if I'm ever going to complain to her, I'll have to remember that week, knowing she'll definitely remind me if I forget about it.

I will grow to love this woman like a sister and a mother. Her temperament is both strong and nurturing. I've already grown used to her inspiring me to give as much as I possibly can. She has a way of motivating you by coming *close* to insulting you but stopping just short.

At some point while I'm complaining about being tired, I give a delivery to the camera that I know isn't my best. Denise calls me on it. "So you feel pretty good about that?" Denise asks me. "You think that's your best?"

"I don't know. Yeah, I think so."

She calls out to the crew around us. "So, guys. Ty feels pretty good about that. He thinks it's his best." She turns to me and asks, "So you *sure* that's your best?"

Now I'm shaking my head with a smile on my face. "No. I think I have one more in me."

"Awesome. We'd love to see that."

Denise is that kind of person, the one who will say, "That's all you got? 'Cause I'm pretty sure you got something better in you." She delivers it as a challenge—as if she's saying the following: "So if this is the last scene you ever do on camera, you're okay with people remembering you by that?"

"No!"

Denise is one of those who works relentlessly to make sure that whatever project she's a part of is the best it can be. One way she does that is to surround herself with what she considers the greatest workers she can find. And if you mess up, she'll call you out. She calls herself out too. She'll be one of the big reasons I stay in TV so long, and why I last on *Extreme* for so many seasons.

So on November 23, 2010, while Denise is at home, training to climb the actual Mount Everest, I'm texting her throughout the day but don't get an answer. I'll soon be shocked to hear she died from a brain aneurysm. She was only forty-one years old.

I'm not sure what's more difficult—flying down to Allentown to attend her open-casket funeral or speaking at the memorial held for her later in December at the Academy of Television Arts and Sciences in Hollywood. Everybody in the business attends the event to celebrate her life. I'm stunned, and I don't deal with death well, but all I can share is the impact Denise made in my life.

Still, there's no way to adequately show the impact she's made on me. Denise gave me more than simple motivation. She lifted my spirits and showed me that anything was possible because she proved it. She didn't just say you can do better; she showed you how. Denise affected everybody she worked with.

This is the story of my life. All throughout it, there are people who come along who make an impact and turn me into the person I now am. I was a different person when I first met Denise. Working with her felt like joining the military. "Failure is not an option" was her mentality every day. When you meet somebody like that and watch them in action, it changes you. "You know I can't do this" was never something you could tell Denise. She would always ask, "How are we going to do this?"

Denise Cramsey would stand up to anything

People like Denise are more than just family. So are many of the people I meet and work with in this crazy industry. They are grainy, gritty, down-in-the-trenches individuals who work harder than you can ever imagine. Denise is one of those people.

I'll never meet a stronger and more determined person with a heart that loves everyone. She took the time to appreciate who you were as a person. She forced me to believe in myself the way she believed in me. For those of us who knew her, let's consider ourselves lucky and never forget her strength, her spirit, and her laugh. I know I won't.

PS: This is a photo I set up to illustrate how this woman was never intimidated by anything or anyone, even a dirty men's room.

"MOTHER'S LITTLE HELPER"

People sometimes ask me who inspired me to become the man I am today. For the most part, I always have a different answer. I say people like Picasso, Warhol, Basquiat, Jeff Koons, Damian Hirst, Banksy. All of them. Artists who became legends in their own time, some who were driven to create not just art but a different way of thinking about it.

They couldn't forsake the addictive need to embrace artistic expression. They were also completely self-made before branding was even a brand. In other words, they were do-it-yourselfers. Some were smart enough to realize they needed a team to pull off art on an extreme, grand scale.

The same could be said of designers and architects like Charles and Ray Eames, Isamu Noguchi, Ludwig Mies van der Rohe, George Nelson, Finn Juhl, and Mari Mako. They all had vision, focus, and ability to create under pressure. These icons gave us functional forms or sculptures that were ahead of their time and still resonate in the modern world today. Yes. I would say these are the people who inspire me to think beyond what seems safe and normal . . . to think outside the box.

Of all those heroes, I realize there is one dynamic figure in my life who has always lived sort of outside the norm. A person whose passion for working, learning, loving, and laughing is matched only by their excitingly infectious, hilarious personality. A person who can help you learn and learn to love yourself at the same time. Making it easier for you to find your passion. All while working a full-time job, going to college, and raising two children. Yes, I'm talking about my mom.

She is the ultimate do-it-yourselfer. She was a wait-ress, a student, a teacher, a parent, a psychologist, a professional, a dancer, a wife, and a mother, all at the same time. The woman can juggle almost anything. (Except cats . . . she's highly allergic.) She's what you might call driven.

My mother came dancing into this world. And no wonder she was attracted to musicians; she started twirling the baton and leading the school marching band as early as grade school. However, she was smart enough to know that dancing as a Rockette at Radio City Music Hall would only get you so far, but a college education . . . now that had legs. Unfortunately, that also meant she would spend most of her life in some type of school. Always going back for a postgraduate this or that. Not to mention her certifications and dissertations—BAs, PHDs, MBAs, BFDs, and occasional UTIs. All those capital letters kept her pretty busy in the DIY category, which meant the family dinner's ETA was always TBD.

All this meant that we kids needed to fend for ourselves in many categories, especially learning to cook at an early age. My mom would set a calendar in the kitchen, indicating which family member would have cooking or cleaning duty on that particular day. This started when we were pretty young. She would say to Wynn and me, "Who needs to buy a dishwasher when we already have two?"

My mom's always been allergic to dogs, but we had two basset hounds anyway. One night when the calendar says I'm in charge of dinner, I check our fridge and see there's nothing to prepare—a common occurrence in our house. So I go upstairs and knock on my mom's door. As I open it, I see she's doing biofeedback, which is a way of mentally lowering your heartbeat to help heal you from the inside. Aka meditation. Aka she's taking a nap. Please . . . biofeedback. Whatever.

"Mom," I whisper, "what am I supposed to cook for dinner tonight?"

She rolls over and mumbles groggily. "There's some fish in the freezer. Just put it in the oven at 350 for thirty-five minutes."

"Okay. Thanks. Enjoy the drooling."

After receiving my directions, I execute the plan. The fish is cooking. The house has a nice aroma. I even make a salad to go with it. After I yell, "Dinner is served," we all sit down at the family table. This is where things get interesting. As my dad begins to slice into the freshly baked fish (which smells quite good), an ominous brown, bile-like fluid begins to seep out of the fish. My brother gags like he's gonna puke, while I, of course, start laughing. My father's not laughing, however. He knows something's a little . . . wait for it . . . fishy.

Yes, Mom forgets to remind me that the fish need to be cleaned. I mean, seriously—who buys a fish with its guts still in it and then just throws it in the freezer for later use? Uh, yeah, that would be my mom. The same person who puts the leftover Thanksgiving turkey in a Ziploc bag and serves it a year later when it's as dry as dust and covered in freezer burn. Yeah. It's safe to say my mom isn't the kind of mom that makes little sandwiches with the crusts cut off. It's more like, "Here's a can of sardines. Now get to school; you're late."

I have to say, though, she was an amazing mom. No, she didn't get the Betty Crocker Award. Nor did she come close to having the crafty, sewing, canning, washing, folding, homemaker mom genes. What she did have was an amazing amount of patience to make sure she gave enough attention to her kids at the end of the day. I mean, going to school full-time while holding two jobs and caring for two kids is enough. Honestly, that woman has had such a positive impact on my life, I can't imagine how I would've turned out if she wasn't raising me. Wait—I probably would've eaten so much better! Ha. But you can't appreciate the easy parts of life until you live through the hard ones.

Mom's always had this incredible way of making you laugh when you're having a really bad day. Laughter, as she told me, is the cure for all that ails you. Which comes in handy during the ice storm of 1977, when all we have is a gas stove and two basset hounds to keep us warm for a week. Whoooooo. Ah, laughter. It really gets you through the cold nights. But I truly think it's tragic moments like these that bring us even closer together as a family. And yes, we all have to sleep on a mattress in front of the gas stove. Together. Just to survive. Now that's a close family.

Speaking of closeness and gas, did I mention that I'm living with my mother again? Oh yeah, you heard it right. I mean, who doesn't want a guy who still lives with his mother? Now let me be clear—she doesn't just live with me; she lives in the room *right next door* to mine. She's become my new alarm clock since I hear all the sounds that come out of her room, and there are a lot of them. Gas? Yep. Sneezes? Yep. Wait . . . Excruciatingly loud sneezes. Like "Oh my Lord, are you okay?" kinds of sneezes. Like the "did you just soil your pants?" sorts of sneezes. "Yep, you did."

So it's pretty relaxing around my place right now. Imagine it—I have a date over, soft music is playing in the background, the lights are dimmed, the mood is romantic, and just as I lean in . . .

"Awwwwwwwchewwwwwwwthhhhhhhhhhhaaaaaarrrrrrrrttttttt!!!"

I smile at my lady as I get up to shut the door. "Oh yeah. Did I mention my mom lives with me?"

Needless to say, the mood changes drastically. And yes, *change* is a word I would say sums up my living situation well. My spare room has changed. The sheets in there are changed regularly, not to mention the Depends diapers. Oh yes, things are changing all the time, including the amount of clutter in the room, as well as the TV channel from sports to God knows what. Thankfully she takes out her hearing aids at night so I can finally just scream at her from the closed door.

Come to think of it, ever since I finally built a beautiful house for my own family, things have really come full circle. I can't help but think of me in that classroom, waging a war of my own making, creating chaos, and then looking up to see her face staring at me. But now it's me peering into her room through the glass window in the door. This time, the look of horror is on *my* face. Peering in at the chaos—clothes thrown over every object, bras and underwear dangling from electronic components that run all the gadgets in a smart home. I see tables full of medication and breathing apparatuses that help lower the sound of snoring.

Yes. Change is in the air. It's almost as if the moment she saw what a nice house I built, she retired. *The next day.* Hmmmm. But let's face it. She took me in when I was a loud, obnoxious, hyperactive pain in the butt. So I owe her a few years of room and board. Wrong word, because we are never bored! Thank goodness for my friend Liz, who keeps an eye on Mom when I'm on the road.

Mom has lots of sayings, but her new one sums up her current state quite well: "It ain't old getting easy."

I'm not going to lie—sometimes I think about bringing Mom the old note she wrote me that asked me to leave the house. Yes, I was only seventeen at the time, and she is seventy-seven now, but if she's not working or going to school, she's got to carry her own weight. Ha.

Yeah. That's what I love about life. You never know what's around the corner, and what I may find in the next home I build. In this case, it's my mom who's waiting for me. And she needs changing. Good times. Now that's when you find out who truly loves you. When you need changing.

Love you, Momma. You are the funniest human I know.

Epilogue

ant to know what life's like with ADHD or ADD? Well, if you've reached this point in the book, then you can picture it pretty well. There are many story lines and sections and soundbites and segments running together.

Success for someone with ADHD is getting to the finish line. Not only that, it's stepping back and looking at the piece in its entirety and realizing there is a method to the madness. Why start at the beginning when your mind has already jumped ahead? Why tell a linear story when life as we know it isn't like that?

Trying to explain what it's like to have ADHD is difficult. For one thing, just trying to stay focused long enough to explain anything is a challenge. That's why it's always entertaining to hear a story told from a mind with ADHD. They sometimes start out already in the heat of the action and then try to backtrack and explain how it all got to this point. Or sometimes they just jump to another story that somehow is triggered in their mind from another word or a SHINY object. This is because we're easily distracted and can start heading down a completely different road that hopefully isn't going to end in a crash-and-burn scenario. All of this I find kind of funny.

I mean, you almost need a handbook to understand and follow the mind of anyone with ADHD. They obviously leap before they look, and that's exactly why they can be so entertaining. This is also why I wanted this book to start not at the beginning but in the middle of chaos. Let's call that chapter 3 or 4 if there were actual chapters. Then putting each section of the book together with puzzling story pieces that ultimately will make sense in the end. That will form a full picture. That's been the goal—that if the reader somehow makes it to the end of this book without getting lost or having to start over, then it makes sense. Then you can begin to understand how the mind of a human with ADHD works.

I think the best way I ever explain ADHD is on a daytime talk show called *The Revolution*. We invite a psychiatrist to help me show what it's like to face the mental challenges of ADHD, so we ask my cohost to play me in a game of Ping-Pong. Then once the challenge of just hitting the ball back across the net is becoming difficult, we have the cohost recite the alphabet . . . backward. It's an amazing visual. He begins to not only miss hitting the ball, but he can't get past the letter *w* before forgetting what comes next. The mind is so overwhelmed and distracted by a bouncing ball that it can't perform the simple task of reciting the alphabet. So it gives up and moves on to something it can do.

That's exactly what it's like living with ADHD. It's trying to focus on completing any task while simultaneously keeping an eye on the ball, but the ball can go running out into traffic. The ball can end up bouncing off a table saw or falling off a building. No wonder when people ask me, "What's your favorite tool?" I always give them the same reply: "My favorite tool is always the camera. It not only captures every moment, thought, and idea, but it's the only thing I know of that has an AUTOFOCUS switch, and that is something you *always* want ON."

I've been fortunate to use that tool a lot in my profession.

Maybe you're struggling to retain the knowledge you're listening to. Maybe everybody else around you is advancing in the book, but you're still stuck in the same paragraph. Then you're lost in the next three pages. Maybe nothing soaks in, even as you're bombarded with facts and figures. Maybe you're so disorganized and so disinformed that you've become so disinterested.

There's always hope, my friend.

Your struggle doesn't have to be ADHD; it can be anything. We saw every form of brokenness and loss on *Extreme*. Those families never gave up hope. They came upon boulders in their path and were forced to change direction. The key is they kept moving.

Life is a never-ending series of buses in front of you that move. The only way to know what's waiting behind them is for you to show up with tools in hand and a whole lotta love in your heart.

BIG TYDEAS/ADIS POZAL IDEAS

✦ I'm going to start building and selling coffin tables. You can put one in your home and put your feet up on it whenever you're watching TV. It's also a great reminder that you need to get off the couch and go live your life. This piece of furniture will make an ideal family heirloom since it's so intricately detailed and designed, but not only that, you get to go inside it at the end of your life! Sure, it's a little expensive, but how *genius* is a coffin table? And how has nobody ever thought of this?

✦ I'm going to create a business called The Organizing Organization. It will be a company that will employ people who help other people become organized.

✦ Parenting idea: Build large storage units out of ottomans that can be used as tables behind your couch or as a hiding place for all the toys and clutter in your house. AND when your kids are getting out of control, you can put your children *in* those storage units for small amounts of time. Let's just call them "Time-Out Zones."